The Power Of You

THE PRACTICE OF BEING ALIVE.

BY C. L. HURT

Disclaimer

This book is intended for educational and informational purposes only. It does not constitute medical, psychological, legal, or professional advice. The author and publisher disclaim any liability for actions taken or not taken based on the contents of this book. Readers are encouraged to consult qualified professionals regarding any physical, mental, emotional, or legal concerns.

Trademark Notice

The Practice of Being Alive™ is a trademark of the author. All other trademarks referenced herein are the property of their respective owners.

Publishing Information

Editorial and Publishing by

Kabeer's Prints Publishing

Camden, New Jersey

United States of America

First Edition

Table of Contents

DEDICATION

For those rebuilding quietly, choosing presence over pressure, and learning how to live on purpose without burning out.

This book is also dedicated to all the friends I lost along the way — those who never had the chance to fully live their lives.

Dosh, Shaun, Ron, Ray, Bino.

And especially to my cousins,

Jamir Syms and **Anjanea Williams**.

Your lives mattered.

Your names are not forgotten.

May the way I choose to live honor the lives you didn't get to finish.

May I stay awake to the gift of being here.

And may everything I build be rooted in gratitude, presence, and truth.

ACKNOWLEDGMENTS

AND THE WINNER IS...

Look, first and foremost—**GOD**. Everything I got, everything I am, everything I'm going to be, that's all You. You the foundation. You the reason. You are the most high, and I move accordingly. Period.

To my mama **Kocsha Hurt**, my grandma **Peggy Freeman**, and my aunt **Regina Hurt**, y'all the real MVPs. The sacrifices y'all made? That's the reason I'm here. Y'all held it down when it was heavy, gave up everything so I could have something. This win right here? This is OUR win. We are champions together.

To my FAMILY, y'all held me down through ALL the chaos. When the world was going crazy and it felt like everything was falling apart, y'all didn't move. Didn't switch up. Didn't fold. Y'all was solid, and that's the type of loyalty you can't buy. We still standing, and that's because of US.

In my DARKEST season, when everything felt impossible, the ones who held me down the most outside my mama were **my sister Damira Hurt**, her fiancé **Tyree Rodgers**, and my brother **Quain Bevans**. Y'all didn't just show up—y'all STAYED. When I was at my lowest, y'all was right there.

That's the type of love that changes everything. That's family for REAL.

To my girl **Giovonni Thompson**, you really held me DOWN. Through everything, you was like "ok, and we win again." That energy and confidence?!? That's what kept me going. You believed when belief was hard to find. You reminded me we were built for this. Reminding me that tough times don't last but strong people do. You a real one, and I'm forever grateful for you.

To my mentors who kept it real with me and didn't gatekeep, y'all opened the doors and gave me the game. Could've kept it to yourself, but you didn't. You saw something in me and chose to pour into it. That's rare. That's royalty. I'm forever grateful for the blueprint.

To everybody who wanted to see me break, who bet against me, who said I wouldn't make it; **THANK YOU**. Your hate was my motivation. Your doubt was my fuel. Y'all tried it, and I still won. This victory tastes even sweeter because of y'all.

To my editor **Charles Alford**, you stuck with me when this thing was still rough. You saw the vision when it was blurry to everybody else. You believed in the story, believed in ME, and rode it out until we got it RIGHT. That's real partnership. That's how champions move.

To my cousin **Lashonda Hurt**, you refused to sign that NDA, wouldn't even read the book until it dropped. That's RESPECT. That's integrity. That's protecting what we are building the right way. You trusted the process and held the line. That's the type of loyalty that lasts forever. Real recognize real.

To my children **Ciani and Jaiden**, y'all SAVED me before I even knew I needed saving. Y'all gave me purpose when I was lost. You're the reason I fought this hard, the reason I never gave up. Every word in this book was written for you. This is YOUR legacy. This is because of y'all. Thank you for being my everything.

To the ones who love me, you guys rode through the FIRE with me. When it got hot, y'all stayed. When it looked impossible, y'all believed. Now we here celebrating, and this moment hits different because y'all in it with me. We did this together.

And after God, I have to thank MYSELF. For never folding and remaining solid when they tried to break me. For getting back up every time they knocked me down. For refusing to be anything less than who I knew I could be. I keep going. I keep fighting. I keep believing. I will keep betting on myself, and I KEEP WINNING.

WE MADE IT.

Pop the champagne, raise your glass

AND THE WINNER IS... US.

INTRODUCTION

THE POWER OF YOU

The Practice of Being Alive

You are not Broken-You are Disconnected

The journey of life has always been about you.

The you that is imperfect, the version that's ready to grow. The version of you that you see when you look in the mirror. The you of today, right now, in this moment. As you are. Just being alive.

Being alive means being present enough to notice. Notice what is happening in your own life. The good, the bad, the ups and downs. It means paying attention to the feelings that show, how your body feels when you are responding instead of reacting and choosing.

Being alive is the difference between moving through your days on autopilot and you creating moments and memories that last.

It is being able to say:

I am here.

It means you are participating in your life, not just surviving it.

Most people do not feel lost in life because they have failed. They feel lost because somewhere along the line they forgot what it means to live. They stopped dreaming, they stopped hoping, and the childlike wonder left.

At all stages of life, it is normal to feel overwhelmed or off-balance. You should not feel ashamed for needing to pause, reset, or refill your cup. Living on purpose does not mean pushing harder — it means learning how to be present without losing yourself in the process.

My journey on this planet has been an interesting one, to say the least. Through love, loss, and life itself, I have learned that balance and peace are not rewards we earn after everything settles. They are choices we practice while life is still happening. The ups and downs are what make the human experience real — and when things feel cloudy, this book is meant to be a light.

Nothing we experience is too big to hold.

When you realize that you have the power to choose how you respond to what is happening, everything begins to shift. Life stops feeling like something that is happening *to* you and starts revealing itself as something unfolding *for* you.

As we learn to accept our losses, embrace our wins, and integrate both into lived wisdom, we give ourselves permission to move forward with clarity instead of pressure.

If you do not choose how, you live your life — who will?

We learned how to function, how to be responsible and how to show up even when our bodies and our spirits said stop.

From the outside, life can look great.

But inside, something feels muted.

This book is for the person who is holding things together — but not feeling fully *here* anymore.

If you have ever thought:

- *I am doing everything I'm supposed to do, so why do I feel like this?*
- *Why does life feel hard even when nothing is technically wrong?*
- *I am not good enough.*

You are not alone.

What is happening is normal and way easier to handle than you think.

At most we were taught how to survive, but how many of us were ever taught how to thrive or how to steady ourselves when we are the ones getting in our own way?

This book is not about changing who you are.

It is about locking in with yourself; gently, practically, and sustainably.

You will learn how life responds:

- to where your attention lives
- to the state of your nervous system
- to the identity you rehearse
- to the standards you tolerate

- to the small actions you repeat

You will notice that life responds to patterns.

And the good news is: patterns can be changed.

This book introduces a simple truth most people miss:

You do not change your life by forcing it.

You change it by practicing a new way of living inside of it.

That is what *The Power of You* is about.

A guarantee that I can make is that this book is not a finish line, nor will you have a miraculous transformation overnight.

This is a daily relationship with yourself that makes life feel worth living again.

You do not need to escape your life to live better. You do not need to become someone else or wait until everything is fixed around you.

You are allowed to live *now*. You can be happy now. You can dream again.

This book will show you how.

A Note on Sound

Some books are written in silence.

This one was not.

The energy of this book lives in the same reflective space as **Moment of Clarity** and **Everything I Am** — not as soundtracks, but as emotional reference points.

Both songs sit in the space between survival and self-definition.

Between knowing who you've been and deciding who you're willing to be next.

They are not loud. They do not perform. They tell the truth without flinching.

You do not need to play them while you read.

But if you know them, you'll recognize the frequency.

How to Use This Book

You can read this book straight through or open it where you feel pulled.

Each chapter introduces one element of the system and ends with a short daily practice. These practices are not tasks. These are check points — subtle ways your body and your life register a shift.

You do not need to do everything right.

You just need to stay honest and consistent.

That is how real practice works.

A Compass You Already Know

In grade school we learned how to understand the world using six questions:

Who. What. When. Where. Why. How.

We were taught to apply them to stories, problems, and assignments —but rarely to ourselves.

This book uses those same questions, turned inward.

- **What is happening?**
  → the **signal** you're receiving
- **Who are you as it happens?**
  → your **internal state**
- **Why does it mean what it means to you**
  → the **? story** being told
- **Where does this live in your life?**
  → your **standards**
- **How do you respond?**
  → your **steps**
- **When do you act — and when do you pause?**
  → your **timing**

You already know how to ask these questions.

This book shows you how to **live inside them.**

The Practice of Being Alive™ Model

Everything in this book is built on this system.

Life responds to six things:

1. Signal

Where your attention goes.

What you feed and track.

Sustained attention quietly organizes your life.

2. State

The condition of your nervous system.

Whether you feel safe, rushed, guarded, or open.

Life does not meet you where you think — it meets you where you are.

3. Story

The language you use.

The identity you rehearse.

The meaning you assign.

Story is not who you are.

It's what you've practiced believing.

4. Standards

What you tolerate.

What you normalize.

What you allow.

Standards are not demands.

They're boundaries.

Life responds to what stays in place.

5. Season

When to act

When to wait

Knowing whether this is a moment for restraint or response.

Understanding the cost of moving too early or too late.

6. Steps

Small, repeated actions.

Not big moves — practiced ones.

Repetition teaches your system what is safe and possible.

When these six are in alignment, life feels more responsive.

When they are not, life feels heavy.

Each chapter addresses one part of this system and shows you how to adjust it **without abandoning yourself**.

This is not about doing more.

It's about staying in flow.

CHAPTER 1

YOU ARE HERE

Waking Up from Autopilot

When did you first start to lose your way? Is there an exact moment that you can pinpoint, or did you wake up one day and realize that something was just off? The truth is you don't lose you way all at once.

You drift.

You drift slowly into adulthood, into surviving, and eventually you drift into doing what is expected of you rather than what feels true.

I know I did.

There was a time in my life where I looked up and everything that I thought I knew about myself, shattered. I was overweight, unmotivated, and surrounded by people who looked nothing like how I wanted my future or even my present moment to look. I was drowning, not in debt, in regret. I questioned, "How could a person with so much promise get here?"

On the outside I looked ok. When you looked at my circle of friends, I was on track; even ahead. I lived on my own, was able to take care of my kids, and I had man that treated me well. I had youth, beauty, and brains. You couldn't tell me anything, I didn't want to hear it.

But one day, something happened. I watched a video and the woman speaking asked a question. She asked,

"Who are you "?

She then said,

"Once you figure that out, ask yourself if that's aligned to who your soul wants to be. Then, see if you're showing up that way."

I stopped the video, and my eyes began to fill with tears.

Her words struck a chord to a silent suffering that was quietly playing in the back of my mind. In an instant, my life flashed before my eyes.

Yes, I was beautiful, but I allowed the man that I was with at the time constantly push me pass my eating limits because "I needed some meat on my bones." And ended up putting on 40lbs and no longer felt comfortable in jeans.

Yes, I lived on my own, but I allowed every friend that had a problem to live with me. When I looked around, I had a rotation of friends and their kids coming in and out. I was able to help everyone else out, but my kids no longer had the security of their own home.

Yes, I had a man that treated me very well, but he wanted more than I had the capacity to give so when he pushed, I pulled. And every day I cried.

So yes, on the outside I looked ok.

In reality,

I was suffering.

Honestly, I was living nothing like what I had envisioned for myself. I did not feel safe. I did not feel secure. Something had to change. Eventually and unconsciously, I began to disengage.

When you begin to disengage with life it looks something like waking up already behind, being frustrated with the people around you and answering messages, making decisions, and moving through the day on autopilot.

But somewhere in the middle of the day, there is a quiet moment where you realize you haven't felt anything yet. No joy, no excitement, nothing out of the ordinary.

By the time you notice it, you don't even think of it as that big of a deal and without paying attention, it later becomes the pattern.

One day you wake up and realize yes, you're functioning, but you're not really living at all.

This isn't a failure on your part, it's a problem with your conditioning.

From an early age, millions of us are taught how to behave, how to adapt, and how to "live" in the real world. We are rewarded for compliance and endurance; society taught us to measure success by productivity instead of fulfillment. We learned to ignore internal cues in favor of external results, and we learned to call feeling stressed out "normal."

Over time, this creates a quiet disconnection from the most

important person on this planet.....YOU.

Not feeling alive does not mean you stop functioning; it means you stop feeling present inside of what you're doing within your life. You stop paying attention to how you show up, not for others, but for yourself.

This is a major reason people confuse the state of being alive with stimulation.

Stimulation is about the feeling from the outside world, it hijacks your nervous system pumping it with adrenaline and urgency. Stimulation makes you feel something for a moment in time.

Feeling alive is about how you respond and about how your body registers what is happening on the inside. Whether what we register is good or bad.

When we stop feeling alive, people often mistake it for depression or lack of motivation, but that's what suppression of life force looks like.

You are not depressed; you're disconnected from yourself. You are still showing up and handling business, all the while, moving like the air has been vacuumed out of your living experience. And just because (in most cases) nothing is visibly wrong with you, the loss is easy to dismiss. Something inside of us never stops noticing though, that subtle feeling; the one that says, *"there has to be more to life than this,"* that isn't you being dissatisfied, it's your soul recognizing that you deserve better.

You did not imagine a fuller life for no reason, and you did not dream it by accident.

Nor did you lose your power. You were simply never taught

how to control it and use it consistently and intentionally.

Life does not respond to wishing, hoping and honorable deeds.
It responds to **rehearsal** and **repetition.**

In layman's terms, life is not a mystery, it is a series of patterns. What we repeat becomes our reality, and the same inputs will keep producing the same outcomes until something in the system changes.

That's it.

This is why some people seem "lucky." They are not blessed, they are aligned.

You may have learned to override your body, bypass your intuition, and push past your limits in the name of success, love, or just surviving. Over time, this creates tension inside the nervous system. And a frazzled nervous system doesn't feel safe growing even when growth is tangible.

This can be uncomfortable because it challenges the PATTERNS that keep YOU safe.

You must learn how to move forward without abandoning your core self.

God did not stop responding to you.

You just stopped responding to yourself.

The spark may feel gone; however, this chapter marks the beginning of turning that connection back on.

Daily Practice: Turning the Signal Back On (5–10 minutes)

1. **Pause the noise (1 minute)**

   Put your phone down. Sit or stand comfortably. Close your eyes, inhale in through your nose and exhale out through your mouth. With each breath, let your shoulders relax more than the time before. Do this five times.

2. **Ask one honest question (2 minutes)**

   Silently or aloud, ask: "*Where in my life am I surviving instead of living?*"

   Do not force an answer. Notice what comes up.

3. **Body check-in (2 minutes)**

   Scan your body quickly:

   - Where do I feel tense?
   - Where do I feel open?

No fixing. Just noticing.

4. **Identity cue (1 minute)**

Say (or write):

"Today, I move as someone who is allowed to enjoy being alive."

5. **One micro-action (same day)**

Do one small thing that supports aliveness:

- Walk without headphones
- Drink water intentionally

- Say no where you normally say yes
- Say yes where you normally hesitate

Nothing dramatic.

CHAPTER 2

LIFE IS RESPONDING, NOT PUNISHING

From Judgement to Feedback

I learned early how to stay alert. Growing up in Camden, you do not move exist casually. You pay attention. You notice moods, shifts, body language and you learn how to read the room to see what is off. My body learned that before I ever thought about it. Even as an adult, I carried that with me.

When I was living in my townhouse, I had a few friends staying with me. One afternoon we were all sitting on the couch, smoking weed, undisciplined, tired, and unmotivated — looking exactly how it felt. My grandmother walked in, looked at us, and went off. She told me I was wasting my life. That I was going to end up with nothing. She was not trying to be mean. She was scared. But the message hit hard. It was not about that day. It was about who I was becoming in her eyes.

I did not argue. I did not defend myself. I absorbed it. After that, I stayed busy. I stopped letting myself slow down. I carried responsibility like proof that I was not what she saw in that moment. I was not that. At some point, slowing down started to feel dangerous. Rest started to feel like ruin. I told myself I was being disciplined, but really, I was trying not to be judged.

Years later, I was standing in my kitchen staring at the sink while the water overflowed onto the counter. Phone in my hand. Tears rolling down my face. Heart racing. Nothing was wrong. I just did not have anything to do. I didn't have a job to do. My kids were off living their lives. Nobody needed me, but me, and still my body was reacting like something bad had just happened. That's when it clicked. My body was responding to old fear — the fear of being seen as lazy, behind, not enough.

The hardest part was realizing how much of my life was shaped by that. I wasn't choosing most days. I was proving something. I wasn't listening for what I wanted. I was listening for what could be used against me. I wasn't overwhelmed, I was just moving through life trying not to end up with nothing.

That moment mattered because it showed me how early messages do not disappear — they settle in. If your body is always trying to outrun judgment, then no amount of success ever feels like enough.

One of the most stressful, exhausting, and victimizing thoughts that you can have is the idea that life is something that is happening *to* you.

That you're being tested.

That you're being punished.

That something keeps "going wrong."

Most people live with a quiet "why me" running in the background. And that mindset slowly robs you of your power. Because if you feel like life is punishing you, then your only options become guilt, fear, or waiting for somebody to save you.

But what if life isn't punishing you at all? What if it's

responding to you?

That shift changes everything. Because when you stop asking what's wrong with you, you can start noticing what's being reflected back on to you. When something doesn't work out, the questions usually come fast:

- Why does this always happen to me?
- What did I do wrong?
- Why does life keep doing this?

Those questions feel natural, but they shut things down. They assume something is broken, either in you or in the world.

But what if neither is true?

What if life isn't against you, just responding to how you move through it?

Punishment vs. Feedback

The idea that life is punishing us didn't come from truth, it came from conditioning. Long before we had language for nervous systems, patterns, or psychology; punishment was used to create order. In families, schools, religions, and ancient societies, punishment was often viewed as the result of doing something wrong and the mindset that if you were wrong then you are obviously bad. Over time, that same thinking became internalized. When something negative happened, the mind learned to ask, *what did I do to deserve this?* Punishment gives pain a reason. It makes suffering feel explainable, even if the explanation hurt.

But the thing is, life doesn't operate on moral judgment. It operates on **response**.

What you repeat isn't what you deserve, it's what's familiar, rehearsed, and then reinforced.

This is where the shift in your mind happens.

Think about it:

If life is punishing you, your only options are guilt, fear, or waiting for someone or something to fix it. But if life is responding to you, you regain leverage. You can observe what's happening, adjust how you move, and choose differently without turning yourself into the problem.

Punishment assumes something is wrong with you.

Responding assumes something can be changed.

That distinction matters because when difficulties are framed as punishment, the nervous system stalls. You brace. You stop experimenting. You stop trusting yourself. But when challenges are seen as feedback, the system flows. You remain engaged. You stay in relationship with yourself and your life instead of pulling away from it.

Life works like a mirror, not a judge.

It reflects patterns — not morality. It responds to expectations, boundaries, your nervous system state, how you talk, and what you repeat. The same internal signals will keep producing the same outcomes until something in the system changes.

That doesn't mean you caused everything that's happened to you. It means that what you rehearse *now* matters more than what happened before.

And once you see that, you stop asking, "*why does this keep happening to me?*"

You start asking, *what is this responding to — and what can I adjust?*

That question returns power to where it belongs.

When life feels punitive, it's easy to take everything on as if it's your fault. You assume every setback means failure. You shut down. Your body tightens. You stop dreaming.

When you shift your perspective to life is giving you constant feedback, you stay engaged.

You observe what's happening. You make minor changes. You keep moving.

Experiences play out like a scene in a movie, showing you what's working and what's not by repeating patterns until something changes.

I'll never forget a woman I met in Atlanta.

Absolutely gorgeous.

Successful.

A beautiful personality.

She came from a prestigious family and carried herself with confidence.

But when we talked, she kept circling back to her relationships.

She told me that for most of her life, she had been in some form of abusive relationship. Emotionally, verbally, sometimes physically. It became familiar. Normal, even.

Then she finally met a good man.

And something unexpected happened.

She became the abuser.

Not because she was cruel. But because chaos felt familiar, and peace didn't.

Every relationship after that began to resemble the very thing she thought she had outgrown.

At first, she saw it as punishment.

Like life was saying, *"This is what you deserve."*

Like no matter how much she healed, she would always end up in the same place.

What changed everything for her wasn't another breakup.

It was a conversation with a friend.

Her friend didn't shame her.

Didn't diagnose her.

Didn't tell her she was broken.

She simply said,

"Maybe this isn't punishment. Maybe it's life trying to show you what you need to heal."

That stopped her.

Because if this was punishment, that would mean something was wrong with her.

But feedback meant something was still being learned.

She realized she had never learned how to feel safe in calm.

She didn't know how to be in love without tension.

Her nervous system had memorized survival — not stability.

Life wasn't punishing her.

It was showing her, again and again, what still needed attention.

Once she saw it that way, the pattern stopped feeling personal.

And when it stopped feeling personal, she could finally change it.

When you stop interpreting challenges as judgment and start seeing them as information, you regain choice, and that choice is where your power lives.

Life works the same way. Situations that feel "stuck" are because the same internal programs keep running in the background.

This doesn't mean you caused everything that's happened to you. That belief can become just another form of self-blame. It means that what you rehearse **now** matters more than what happened before.

And that's the crazy thing about life...in order to live it fully, you have to be held accountable.

Accountability is about leverage and leverage is freedom.

Accountability vs Responsibility

Accountability isn't about right or wrong. It's about ownership. Responsibility is how you choose to act once that ownership is yours.

For many of us, our first experience with accountability didn't happen at work or in relationships — it happened in our families. And in most families, accountability wasn't taught as responsibility. It was taught as blame. Someone did something wrong. Someone needed to explain themselves. Someone needed to feel bad enough to change.

Mistakes weren't treated as information. It was treated as proof that something bad had occurred or that trouble was on the way.

So, accountability became something to fear.

In my family, responsibility, was rarely explained. We weren't taught how to respond to what happened — we were taught how to manage the emotional fallout of it. I was taught to keep the peace and to not rock the boat so things don't fall apart.

That's how many people learned to handle responsibility.

They learned to:

- over-explain.
- over-apologize.
- over-function
- take emotional ownership for things they didn't cause.

Not because you're mature but because it keeps your system stable.

This is where the distinction matters.

Accountability, when distorted, says:

"This is your fault."

Responsibility, when healthy, says:

"This is what I can change."

Accountability tied to shame teaches the nervous system that mistakes cost connection and somehow makes you bad. Responsibility teaches the nervous system that choice still exists.

Responsibility is leverage. It's the moment you stop arguing with what happened and start choosing how you move forward. It doesn't ask you to take on guilt. It asks you to stay present.

You can acknowledge impact without taking on shame.

You can change behavior without believing you're broken.

You can take responsibility without abandoning yourself.

Most of us weren't taught that at home.

So you're learning it now.

Why Responsibility Feels Heavy (Until It Doesn't)

Responsibility sometimes sounds like pressure, like more to manage, and like more stress. That's because responsibility is often taught without compassion. Responsibility feels heavy when it's confused with blame.

When responsibility carries shame, the body tightens. You brace. You rush to fix. You over-explain. You feel like you're carrying the weight of the outcome *and* the weight of your worth at the same time.

That's not responsibility — that's self-punishment.

Real responsibility is lighter than people expect because it isn't about carrying everything. It's about identifying what's **actually yours to adjust** and putting the rest down.

The moment responsibility feels overwhelming, pause and ask:
What part of this is mine — and what part am I taking on out of habit?

You don't have to absorb guilt to take responsibility.

You don't have to collapse to be accountable.

You don't have to fix everything to move forward.

Responsibility becomes manageable when it's specific.

Being responsible feels heavy when you try to carry outcomes, emotions, and identity all at once. It feels lighter when you separate them. You acknowledge what happened, decide what you'll do next, and release the rest.

Taking responsibility doesn't mean standing in the wreckage. It means choosing one adjustment and staying present long enough to make it.

And when responsibility is practiced this way — without shame, without urgency — it stops feeling like a burden and starts feeling like movement.

Once you understand that life responds to:

- Expectations
- Boundaries
- Nervous system state

- Language
- Repetition

you'll stop waiting for permission to feel better.

You stop fighting yourself for not having it "figured out."

The Loop That Keeps People Stuck

Many people live inside the same loop for years, they feel overwhelmed and disconnected.

They push harder or shut down and when nothing really changes, they get frustrated and decide that life is unfair.

Then the cycle restarts.

There's an old commercial I think about sometimes.

A man can't get a job because he doesn't have experience.

He can't get experience because he didn't go to school.

And he can't go to school because he doesn't have a job.

It makes sense but it goes nowhere.

That's a loop.

Accountability looks for fault whereas responsibility looks to replace the one small action or thought that will break the loop. This loop isn't caused by laziness or lack of effort. It's caused by misalignment. And effort without alignment creates exhaustion while effort with alignment creates active motion.

Why the Body Matters More Than You Think

Here's where most advice falls short.

Life doesn't just respond to what you *think.*

It responds to what your body is broadcasting.

This is why you can't think your way into a better situation, your body has to change its frequency too.

A nervous system that feels unsafe reads neutral situations as threats. It reacts quickly, defensively, or shuts down entirely. Even good opportunities can feel overwhelming when the body doesn't feel settled enough to receive them.

I once saw a demonstration showing how different emotional states affect the space around a person. Calm, grounded emotional states felt expansive. Tense, guarded states felt contained. The experiment essentially showed that when the nervous system feels safe, the body opens up. You take up space without effort. When the nervous system is under threat, everything contracts. Energy pulls inward and your focused on protection.

It wasn't magic or mysticism it was science.

Your life responds does the same and this is why "thinking positive" does not work on its own. The body must feel included. We have to learn how to **regulate first — then respond**. You can't force real change. It happens when what you think, feel, and do match.

How to Read Your Life Differently

Once you see life as responsive, you start asking what I like to call *empowering questions.*

Not: *Why is this happening to me?*

But:

- What keeps repeating here?
- What signal might I be sending without realizing it?
- What small adjustment would change the direction of this?

These questions don't overwhelm you. They bring you back to where your power actually lives, in choice. Real choices, made consistently, are what change trajectories.

You're Not Behind

When people start noticing patterns, regret usually follows. "*I should have known this sooner. Why did it take so long?*"

Let that go.

My advice is simple: forgive yourself for not knowing what only time could teach you.

Awareness doesn't arrive early or late. It arrives when you're ready to use it.

If you're reading this, you're no longer just reacting to life. You're beginning to participate in it. That's the shift.

Life doesn't require perfection. It responds to honesty, consistency, and small corrections made daily. You don't need to change everything. You need to change one thing at a time.

Little things become big things.

That's how momentum builds.

Daily Practice: Reading the Feedback (5–10 minutes)

1. **Name the pattern (2 minutes)**
   Choose one area of your life that feels repetitive or

stuck.
Ask: *What keeps showing up here?*

Don't analyze. Just notice.

2. Check the state (2 minutes)

When this pattern appears, how does your body usually feel?

- Tight
- Rushed
- Guarded
- Shut down

Awareness comes before change.

3 Language shift (2 minutes)

1. Replace:

"Why does this always happen to me?"

With:\"What is this responding to — and what can I adjust?"

4 One small shift (same day)

Choose one micro-adjustment:

- Pause before responding.
- Hold a boundary.
- Slow down one decision
- Take one regulating breath.

Small shifts change signals.

Changed signals change outcomes.

CHAPTER 3

SIGNAL

Where Your Attention Lives

Most people think money runs the world. It doesn't. **Attention does.** Money, Opportunities, relationships, and even your sense of self follows attention. Where your attention goes, your life quietly organizes itself around it.

Our lives aren't shaped around intention. We build them around attention. Whatever you feed yourself (what you watch, listen to, and take in) the most starts shaping what feels normal and whatever you keep going back to keeps getting reinforced.

Social media is a perfect example of this. You pause on one type of content — stare or compare, indulge in drama — and suddenly that's all you see. Not because that's all there is, but because the algorithm teaches the system what to deliver.

Life works the same way.

If your attention lives in worry, you feel on edge.

If you focus on comparison, you feel behind.

If you put all your attention into managing others, you disappear.

Attention becomes structure and that structure becomes your reality because attention goes where attention flows.

You're Always Paying for Something

Every day, you're spending attention — whether you realize it or not.

On worry.

On replaying conversations that already ended.

On scrolling past other people's lives while ignoring your own.

When I realized that this was happening to me, I found meditation, Meditation didn't make me calm.

It made me honest and it taught me how to intentionally focus. When everything got quiet, I realized how little of my life I was actually in. My body was present, but my attention was everywhere else, ahead of me, behind me, rehearsing, preparing.

I wasn't living in the moment, and I wasn't really experiencing life.

My attention was split between what already happened and what I was afraid might happen next.

Old conversations. Imagined outcomes. Invisible emergencies.

Meditation didn't bring new thoughts.

It exposed the story I'd been living inside of.

It was like finally turning the lights on in a room that I'd been walking through in the dark. The Johnny Nash song "I Can See Clearly Now" became my theme song. That's when everything shifted. "I can see clearly now; the rain is gone" became the line that named what I'd been missing — perspective.

I finally understood what we give our attention isn't neutral ground, It's an emotional investment.

Whatever holds your attention is shaping how safe your body feels.

Whatever your body feels, it starts preparing for.

And whatever you prepare for... you begin to live inside of.

I wasn't stuck because I lacked discipline or belief.

I was stuck because my attention never stayed anywhere long enough to let me feel grounded.

That's why attention is currency.

Every day, you spend it on something.

Worry. Protection. Comparison. Or presence.

And over time, life gives you more of whatever you keep paying for.

Attention is not infinite, and it is not neutral. Your attention is the currency of energy exchange. Some payments compound. Others drain. Most people are exhausted not because they're doing too much — but because their attention is constantly being pulled away from themselves.

Why Attention Won't Stay

People say they're overwhelmed but in reality, they are scattered. You don't feel scattered because you can't focus. You feel scattered because your attention doesn't stay in one place long enough to let anything catch. When your nervous system is used to being alert, you subconsciously move your mind to what feels safe. Not from distraction but from protection.

Attention that never lands can't build momentum, and life starts to feel rushed, thin, and disconnected.

Feeling scattered isn't a flaw it's something to pay attention to, because it means your current circumstances aren't allowing your nervous system to feel safe. And when you don't feel safe, your brain can't connect. When safety returns, you able to focus on what you want without force.

When your attention is split in too many directions, your energy leaks.

You start:

- Starting things but not finishing
- Thinking about change but not acting
- Wanting clarity but never feeling settled enough to do anything about it.

Not because you're incapable — but because your attention never stays anywhere long enough to build momentum.

Nothing grows where attention doesn't linger.

Think about a houseplant.

At first, you buy it with good intentions.

You place it by the window.

You water it for a week or two.

Then life gets busy.

You stop noticing the soil.

You forget to rotate it toward the light.

You don't see the leaves drooping because you're not looking anymore.

The plant doesn't die immediately.

It just... stalls.

No new growth.

No vibrancy.

Not because the plant is broken.

Not because you did something wrong.

It simply isn't being invested in.

Attention is the currency.

Water, light, and care are how that currency gets spent.

What you don't look at doesn't grow.

What you don't check in with doesn't evolve.

What you don't invest attention into stays exactly where it is.

The grass only looks greener on the other side of the fence because you're looking over there. Start tending to your own garden.

What You Rehearse Feels Normal

Here's what you need to understand.

What you pay attention to becomes familiar. What's familiar starts to feel normal. What feels normal shapes identity. And identity quietly determines what you experience.

- If your attention is consistently on:
- Lack → you begin to expect it.
- Chaos → you brace for it.
- Other people's needs → you disappear.
- Fear-based information → you stay on edge.

Your system adapts to survive in that environment.

But attention can be redirected.

When your attention is on:

- Stability → you begin to expect support.
- Order → you move with more ease.
- Your own needs → you stay present.
- Truth-based information → you remain calm.

Your identity shifts accordingly.

That's how attention fuel's identity — not through effort, but through repetition.

Why the World Is Competing for Your Focus

Your attention is valuable — and not just to you.

Entire industries are built on keeping you distracted, reactive, emotionally stimulated, and slightly dissatisfied. Because a distracted person is easier to influence. A reactive person is easier to sell to. An insecure person scrolls longer.

It's called the *attention economy*, companies design apps, feeds, and notifications to pull your focus again and again because every second you're engaged is another second they can monetize.

If every time you login your noticing "hey I was just talking about this" or "I think my phone is listening to me." This isn't paranoia. They are paying attention so why aren't you?

If you don't decide where your attention goes, something or somebody else will.

Attention Is How You Signal to Life

Attention is one of the main ways we tell our brain what matters and what doesn't. When your able to pay attention to something long enough, your system settles. Things start to make sense and feel more connected.

When your attention is constantly being pulled, those signals get scattered. The body stays on edge, never relaxing always waiting for the next thing. Even meaningful moments can pass by without really sticking. Over time, you can begin to feel distant — not because you are but because your attention never stays in one place long enough to let you feel it.

Life and energy respond to where you place sustained focus. Sustained focus is the ability to stay with one thing long enough for depth to form.

This is why people who "look like they have it all" often just have better attention boundaries. They're not everywhere, constantly reacting and they're not consuming without intention.

They choose where their attention lives — and protect it.

Why Simplicity Compounds

There's a pattern you'll notice among many extremely successful people.

They simplify the things that *don't matter*

so they can protect attention for what does.

Some wear the same style of clothing every day.

Some eat the same meals over and over.

Some structure their mornings almost identically, no matter how much money they make.

From the outside, it can look boring.

But it's strategic.

Every choice you make costs attention.

What to wear.

What to eat.

When to start.

How to respond.

Most people spend their best mental energy deciding things

that don't actually move their lives forward.

High-level performers do the opposite.

They remove friction where it isn't needed so attention can be spent where it matters like timing, people, and their chosen direction.

Attention is currency don't waste it on things that don't compound.

Reclaiming Your Attention Changes Everything

Once you start paying attention to what you pay attention to, things will begin to shift.

You'll begin to notice your own thoughts again.

You'll feel your energy body more clearly.

You make better decisions faster.

Your reactions soften.

You stop chasing and start choosing. Vigilance isn't required; intention is. That's how momentum builds — not by doing more, but by leaking less. Power doesn't come from forcing motivation. It comes from containment. When your attention has a place to land, energy returns on its own, and life starts to feel workable again.

Daily Practice: Attention Audit (5–10 minutes)

1. Notice the drain (2 minutes)

Today, notice what pulls your attention away from yourself most often:

- A person

- A thought loop
- An app
- A worry

Just notice. No judgment.

2. **Choose one boundary (same day)**

Pick one small boundary:

- No phone for the first 10 minutes of the day
- Pause before opening an app.
- Finish one task before starting another.

Small containment builds power.

3. **Redirect once (real time)**

When you catch your attention drifting, gently bring it back to what you're doing.

That's it.

Attention strengthens through practice — not control.

4. **Close the loop (1 minute)**

At the end of the day, ask:

Where did my attention live today?

That question alone begins the shift.

CHAPTER 4

STATE

Your Nervous System Sets the Ceiling

The first time I went to California wasn't for fun. It was for a Lisa Nichols mastermind in Newport Beach — the wealthiest city in the state. From the moment I arrived, my body knew it was different. The room was filled with multi-millionaire women who looked like me. Confident. Composed. Successful. And for reasons I couldn't explain yet, they kept gravitating toward me. They wanted to talk. They wanted to connect. They wanted to know what I was building.

Instead of feeling affirmed, I panicked.

I remember stepping away and crying. Not quietly — fully overwhelmed. I called my cousin and told her I didn't feel good enough to be there. That I was out of my depth. That I should leave before I embarrassed myself. Nothing bad had happened. No one had rejected me. But my body was reacting like I'd crossed a line I wasn't allowed to cross.

She didn't let me run. She told me to wipe my tears and go back into the room. She said, *who deserves this more than you?* I didn't suddenly feel ready. I didn't feel confident. I just stopped trying to escape the moment.

And when I walked back in, something shifted. I stayed. I spoke. I took up space. Not because I had finally believed I belonged — but because I didn't leave when my body told me to shrink. That experience showed me something I couldn't unsee. Wanting more was never my issue. Being safe enough to hold it was.

That was the first time I understood the ceiling wasn't outside of me. It was internal. And it wasn't about worth — it was about capacity.

I can remember another time a few years ago, everything was falling apart.

I had a lot of friends who weren't friends. My employees were disgruntled and stealing. Contractors I hired were lying. And the man I was dating was toxic in ways I would never admit because I loved him.

My body knew. Hell, my life knew. I kept getting red flags I refused to acknowledge.

One day my aunt flew in for a few hours. He wanted to meet her, but the scheduling just didn't work out.

After I dropped her off at the airport, her return flight got canceled. So, I immediately turned around and picked her back up then we decided to go to dinner.

That's when my daughter called.

"Mom, I just saw a man running out of the house."

Before she could even finish her description, I knew exactly who it was.

I called him. No answer. Then the texts started coming in, calling me everything but my name, accusing me of lying about my aunt being there and projecting what he was doing onto me.

And I'm sitting across from her at dinner.

I couldn't let her see me upset. So, I smiled, I ate, and I texted back as if nothing was wrong. Like my world wasn't collapsing in real time.

She asked me was everything all right as she watched me text rapidly but in silence.

Maybe she recognized it. A silent strength in the broken women who came before us.

I nodded and continued smiling saying "yes" lightly.

After dinner, I rushed her to her hotel and drove back to Jersey.

I got on the bridge. No other cars. Just me and the dark.

Two guys pulled up asking why I was driving so slowly. I looked, laughed, and kept going.

Then out of nowhere my car started spinning.

I wasn't speeding. I wasn't distracted. I was just... spinning. I hit the median. Then I just sat there waiting for someone to come.

And nobody ever showed up.

So, I picked up my bumper and I drove home.

He'd stolen my passport, my other phone and flew to Vegas. I was pissed.

I sat in my bed that night thinking about every aspect of my life and it came to me clear as day.

The car didn't spin because I did something wrong.

It was divine intervention showing me that my life was spinning out of control.

My body had been holding everything I couldn't say out loud; the abuse, the lies, the chaos I kept calling normal. I'd sat calm at that table with my aunt, while my chest tightened, and my hands shook.

When I got on that bridge alone, with nobody left to perform for, my world said *enough.*

The spinning wasn't the first warning. It was just the one I couldn't dismiss.

You can override your signals for a while but your body keeps score, and eventually, it makes you listen. Not as punishment but as a show of protection.

In Newport Beach, my body couldn't hold opportunity.

On that bridge, my body couldn't hold chaos.

The ceiling worked both ways.

For a long time, I thought if I just understood enough, things would finally change. If I went to the conference, if I just stayed positive, if I didn't let myself feel down. I thought things would automatically change.

From the outside, it looked like I was doing everything "right." Inside, my soul was exhausted.

Every time things started to open up for me; an opportunity, momentum, a sense of relief, I felt nothing. Just numb.

I didn't know what it was then. I just knew I couldn't relax.

What I eventually realized was, my life wasn't stuck because I didn't want more; my body didn't feel safe holding more, good or bad.

That realization changed everything.

Desire vs Capacity

We talk a lot about desire. We don't talk nearly enough about **capacity**.

I wanted ease, but my body was used to pressure.

I wanted stability, but my system was wired for chaos.

I wanted things to feel lighter, but I didn't trust lightness to last.

So even when good things showed up, I sabotaged them.

If this feels familiar, I want to say this clearly:

There is nothing wrong with you.

Your nervous system learned how to survive, and it learned well.

It learned to anticipate, to prepare, to stay one step ahead of disappointment.

When I was a kid, I was used to getting the roles I wanted in school. Plays, presentations. and all kinds of opportunities.

It felt normal. I showed up, I tried, and things usually worked out.

Until third grade.

I auditioned for the lead in a school play and didn't get it. I remember the disappointment vividly.

I locked myself in a closet.

Not because anyone told me to, not because something terrible had happened; But because my body didn't know where to put that feeling.

It was the first time I had wanted something, reached for it, and been told no. And my nervous system didn't have a map for that yet. So, it reacted the only way it knew how — by hiding.

No one taught me how to process disappointment.

No one showed me how to stay present with rejection and still feel safe.

So, my body learned something that day:

Avoid this.

Not consciously.

Instinctively.

After that, I stopped putting myself in situations where rejection was likely. I stayed where I already felt capable. I chose spaces where the outcome felt predictable.

From the outside, it could have looked like confidence.

Inside, it was regulation.

That moment didn't define my ability — it shaped my tolerance.

And that's how ceilings form.

Not from lack of talent.

Not from failure.

But from moments our nervous system hasn't learned how to survive yet.

You can want more.

You can be ready for more.

But until the body learns that disappointment, rejection, and uncertainty are survivable, it will quietly guide you back toward what feels safe.

The ceiling is set by your nervous system, not your ambition. I wasn't taught how to grow without expecting chaos. And unless you grew up like Blue Ivy Carter—who said she ain't never seen a ceiling in her whole life—I'm guessing you weren't either.

Where Limits Actually Live

I started paying attention to when my body reacted — not when things were bad, but when they were good.

Compliments made me uncomfortable.

Rest felt undeserved.

Support felt like something I had to earn.

I couldn't do anything well without the anxiety that would get from every compliment that felt like it deserved a better home.

That's when it started to make sense.

The ceiling wasn't on the outside of me, it was internal.

My system had a limit for how much ease, attention, and support it could tolerate before it snapped back into control mode.

Once I saw that, I stopped trying to push past it.

I started learning how to **raise it.**

What Safety Really is

I used to think regulation meant being calm.

It doesn't.

Regulation means:

- You can feel intensity without abandoning yourself.
- You can pause without panicking.
- You can receive without immediately preparing for loss.

Regulation means feeling safe. Sometimes regulation feels boring, and it can sometimes feel unfamiliar. But it's the only way real change lasts. Change doesn't stick when it only lives in your head. It sticks when your body agrees.

Raising Capacity Without Force

Nothing shifted overnight. What shifted were small moments. Letting myself rest and not explaining why. Saying no and letting the discomfort pass. Allowing something to go well without waiting for it to fall apart.

Each time, my body took notes.

Oh. We're safe here.

That's how the ceiling moved — inch by inch.

And as it did, my life responded differently.

Things started meeting me where I actually was.

Why This Matters More Than Mindset

You can believe all the right things and still feel stuck if your body is operating from survival.

This is why people say:

"I know better, but I still react the same."

It's not a mindset issue.

It's a capacity issue.

You can't receive peace if your system thinks peace means danger.

You can't hold abundance if your body associates more with collapse.

Raising your ceiling doesn't mean forcing expansion, it means building safety slowly enough that your body trusts it.

This Is What No One Tells You

You were probably taught how to go for the things that you want but very few of us are taught how to receive. Receiving requires safety; Safety requires regulation and regulation requires practice, not perfection.

You don't need to heal everything before life improves. You need to stop asking your body to hold more than it knows how to.

And then teach it. Gently. Consistently.

Daily Practice: Raising the Ceiling

Today, notice one moment when things feel a little lighter — or when they could.

Instead of rushing past it, pause.

Take one slow breath and tell yourself:

"I'm allowed to be here."

That's enough for today.

CHAPTER 5

SEASON

Before You Move

Just because you can do something doesn't mean you should.

Most of us aren't taught that. We're taught that open doors mean invitations. That hesitation equals doubt. That stopping means giving up.

So we move faster than we're ready.

What I didn't learn is how much timing actually matters, or how often life becomes harder simply because we acted in the wrong season.

Scripture says it plainly:

There is a time for everything, and a season for every activity under the heavens.

A time to plant and a time to uproot.

A time to build and a time to tear down.

A time to speak and a time to be silent

There's no judgment in that list. No hierarchy. Nothing promises that one season is somehow better than another. It just shows that different seasons require different responses and confusing them creates unnecessary chaos.

I didn't always respect that principle. I know what it costs to ignore the season you're in because I've paid the price for it over and over.

I was in a season of recovery when the opportunity came.

Not the healing kind. The scrambling kind.

One of the girls that I considered an associate at the time, her son had stolen money from me. A significant amount of money. The kind that doesn't just disappear without consequence, especially where I'm from. It was during a time where I was trying to solidify myself, build something legitimate, something stable. But now I also needed to recuperate what had been taken. Two needs pulling in opposite directions: the long game and the immediate gap.

That's when the application landed in front of me.

The moment I handed it in, I had a vision. Clear as anything. I saw myself in a heist. Money coming in fast, but chaos right behind it. Sirens in the distance. People scattering. The kind of scene where no one walks away clean.

I should've walked away right then.

But I didn't trust what I'd just seen. I told myself it was nerves, overthinking, fear dressed up as intuition. And I wanted to believe the people I was meeting were decent enough not to destroy themselves. I wanted to believe that I was too. So I moved forward.

We made money.

And hell followed.

Betrayal. Greed. Pain. Loss that went deeper than dollars.

Then the IRS criminal investigation unit called me.

I'd stayed out that night. My phone rang, and the voice on the other end was flat, professional, final.

"We're at your house. We need to talk."

My kids weren't home, but that didn't matter. They'd been *at my house*. Looking. Waiting. The place where my children slept, where we ate dinner, where I'd built something I thought was untouchable—reduced to an address on an investigation file.

I remember calling my kids later. Trying to keep my voice steady. Trying to explain something I didn't fully understand yet myself. My daughter asked if we were going to be okay.

I told her yes.

I wasn't sure I was telling the truth.

Everything I'd built was suddenly in jeopardy. My reputation. My business. My family's sense of safety. Not because I was a bad person. Not even because I made an unwise decision in isolation.

This all happened because I made a move in the wrong season.

I was trying to recover what was stolen while simultaneously building something stable. But a season of recovering losses is not the same as a season of building something new. One requires caution, rest, recalibration. The other requires clarity, energy, and solid ground beneath you.

I was trying to do both at once.

So when the vision came, I couldn't afford to see it. I *needed* the opportunity to work. I needed it to close the gap, to get me back on track. That need made me vulnerable. It made me override my own common sense.

What I learned is this: if I see it, it's real. The vision wasn't a warning to question—it was information to act on.

I also learned to read the fine print and stop taking people at their word just because I want to believe they're good. I don't owe anyone the benefit of the doubt at my own expense.

But the biggest lesson was the one that became this chapter: **just because you can do something doesn't mean you should.**

The right opportunity at the right time can change your life.

The right opportunity in the wrong season, especially when you're operating from a place of need instead of readiness, can cost you everything you're trying to protect.

Timing isn't just about when the door opens.

It's about whether you're in the right season to walk through it.

The Ground You're Standing On

Here's what makes recognizing your season so difficult: past seasons don't just disappear.

Being under pressure for a long time teaches you to rush. Living in unstable conditions makes normal feel temporary.

Constantly being in reaction mode makes peace feel uncomfortable.

A lot of times you're still moving based on where you've been, not where you are. That's how people end up rushing or freezing.

This is where timing and season meet.

Timing is the moment you're choosing.

Season is the ground you're standing on.

You might pick the right moment but be standing on unstable ground. Or you might be on solid ground but move before the moment's ready.

Which Season Are You Still Living In?

The season you came from shapes how you see the one you're in.

If you spent years in survival mode, you'll interpret rest as risk. If you're used to being disappointed, you'll read opportunity and help as a setup. If you had to prove yourself constantly, you'll struggle to believe you're already enough.

That's not wrong. That's pattern recognition doing what it's supposed to do, keeping you safe based on what used to be true.

The problem is when your reality has shifted but your body hasn't caught up.

You're no longer in the season that taught you to move that way, but you're still moving that way. You're reacting to a reality that doesn't exist anymore, which means you're out of sync with the one that does.

So, before you decide what to do next, you have to ask: Am I responding to this season, or the last one?

If you're rushing because scarcity trained you to grab what's available, that's the old season talking. If you're hesitating because past mistakes made you distrust yourself, that's the old season too.

The work isn't to erase what you learned. It's to recognize when it's no longer serving you. Use what you learned to empower you not to hinder you and keep you stuck.

Not Ready vs. Not Willing

There's a difference between "I'm not ready" and "I'm scared to move."

Not ready sounds responsible. It sounds wise. But sometimes it's just another way of saying you don't trust yourself yet, and you're waiting for a level of confidence that doesn't come before you start.

So how do you know which one you're in?

Not ready feels like something's actually missing. You don't have the resources yet. The foundation isn't stable. The people or systems you'd need aren't in place. There's a real gap between where you are and what the next step requires.

Not willing feels like everything's in place but you. The path is clear, the timing is right, but you keep finding reasons to wait. You say you're being careful, but really, you're rehearsing failure. You're preparing for disappointment before you've even tried.

If you can't tell the difference, ask: What would need to be true for me to feel ready?

If the answer is specific and actionable, "I need three more months of savings" or "I need to finish this project first," you're probably not ready yet.

If the answer is vague or endless, "I need to feel more confident" or "I just need to know it'll work out," you're not waiting on readiness. You're waiting on guarantees that don't exist.

And that's when waiting stops being preparation and starts being avoidance.

Just as moving too fast has a cost, staying in place too long does too.

There are seasons where preparation has done all it can do. Where waiting doesn't bring more clarity, it makes you restless. Where you're not protecting yourself anymore, you're postponing yourself.

You can feel the difference.

What Productive Waiting Feels Like

When you're waiting in the right season, it doesn't feel passive. It feels active in a quieter way.

You're building something. Learning something. Letting something settle. There's movement even if it's not visible yet. You're preparing the ground, not just standing on it.

The discomfort is manageable because you know what you're waiting for. You're not stalling, you're getting ready. And when the moment comes, you'll recognize it.

Productive waiting has direction. It has purpose. It might be slow, but it's not stuck.

What Postponing Feels Like

Postponing feels different.

The pause stops feeling calm and starts feeling like you're wasting time. You revisit the same thoughts without learning anything new. Nothing is really changing. Nothing is sticking. The discomfort is not about waiting anymore, it's about not moving.

You're no longer preparing. You are repeating. You're convincing yourself you need one more thing, one more sign, one more guarantee before you can start, but the truth is, you've been ready. You've just been unwilling to find out what happens next. That restlessness you feel. That's not doubt. That is potential that you're refusing to act on.

When preparation and timing come together, your body knows before your mind does. The question stops being "Am I ready?" and becomes "What am I waiting for?"

If you do not have a clear answer, you're probably postponing.

Scripture says:

God has made everything beautiful in its time.

Not early.

Not late.

In its time.

Forcing something before it's ready doesn't improve it, it makes it heavier. But ignoring the moment when it is ready does the same thing.

Your seasons aren't about delay, they're about alignment.

The Questions That Change

Knowing what season you're in changes the questions you ask.

You stop asking, Can I do this?

And start asking, Should I?

Just because you can doesn't mean you should, at least not yet.

And just because you've been waiting doesn't mean you should keep waiting.

Season teaches both restraint and response.

Sometimes the wisest move is to stop.

Sometimes it's to move cleanly, without delay.

Discernment is knowing the difference.

And that discernment starts with one honest look: What is this season actually asking of me? Not what I wish it were asking. Not what it asked last time. What it's asking now.

After You Know Your Season

Recognizing your season is one thing. Acting on it is another.

Once you know where you are, whether you're in preparation, transition, or the moment to move, the next question isn't what to do. It's how you're going to honor it.

If you're in a season of preparation, the question becomes:

What do I need to stop doing so I can actually build what's next? Preparation doesn't mean researching endlessly or constantly second guessing yourself. Being prepared means creating the conditions that make movement possible when the time comes.

If you're in a season of transition, the question is: What am I willing to let go of so I have room for what's coming? Transition requires release. You can't carry everything from the last season into the next one. Something has to stay behind.

If you're in a season of movement, the question is: Am I moving because it's time, or because I'm uncomfortable staying still? Movement for its own sake creates just as much friction as waiting too long. The goal isn't constant motion, it's aligned action.

Honoring your season means you stop fighting it. You stop wishing you were somewhere else. You stop rushing what needs time or delaying what's already ready.

You work with the season you're in, not against it.

And when you do that, the next question becomes unavoidable: What am I willing to tolerate, and what has to change?

Practice

This week, notice when you're about to move forward with something.

Before you do, ask yourself:

Is this the right season for this, or am I just reacting to the opportunity being available? Then ask:

If I wait, what am I protecting? If I move now, what am I

risking?

The answer doesn't need to come immediately. Sometimes clarity takes a few days to surface. But the question itself will shift how you move.

CHAPTER 6

STORY

The Identity That's Running the System

You have probably had a moment, when you realized something isn't right. You're doing everything you were told to do. You're trying. You are holding it together. And still, the same patterns keep showing up just dressed differently.

Different job, same stress.

Different relationship, same disappointment.

Different year, same feeling.

That is usually when people blame circumstances. They blame their parents. Their environment. Their relationships. And sometimes those things matter but they are not telling the full story.

The harder truth is this: your life isn't responding to what you want. It is responding to how you are showing up inside it. The beliefs that you are carrying. The tension you live with. The way your body meets opportunity and pressure.

Nothing is wrong with you. But something in you keeps repeating what it knows. And until that changes, the outcomes will not change either.

Tabula Rasa

There is a theory called *tabula rasa.* It means "blank slate." The idea is simple: we are not born with a fixed identity. We are born without a story about who we are or how life works. Your identity is formed. Your identity is written over time, through experience, through what we are rewarded for, what we are corrected for, and what we must do to get by.

Whether or not you agree with the theory completely is not the point. What matters is this: a large part of what you call *"who I am"* was formed long before you were consciously choosing.

You learned how to respond to stress and what felt safe to expect. You learned what love was and what it is supposed to look like. You learned what effort means and you learned when speaking up was appropriate and when it was time to stay quiet. Some of this was taught directly. Most of it was learned through figuring it out.

Your identity is not who you are at your core. It is who you learned to be to function.

Once an identity trait is learned, it starts running automatically. That is why you can want change and still move the same way when you are tired, pressured, or uncertain. Because identity is the system in control.

Most of us did not choose who we would become. We adjusted. We became the person who kept things moving, who avoided conflict, who held things together, who stayed capable. That version of you may have been exactly who was needed at the time. It may have kept you safe. It may have even helped you survive.

But survival identities do not step aside on their own.

They keep running in the background, long after the environment has changed. And one day, you are no longer in crisis, but you are still living from a way of being shaped by it.

If Chapter 2 showed you that life responds to signals, this chapter shows you where those signals come from.

Awareness does not stop these patterns. It lets you catch them. From here, the work is simple: notice when you are moving from automation and stop long enough to make a different choice. This is where the practice begins, not as effort or self-correction, but as interruption. Small moments where your attention returns and the system updates.

Who Decides When Your Tired

There is the version of you that has dreams, and then there is another version that makes decisions when you are tired, triggered, scared, or unsure. That second one, that is the controller. It is the one who running the show, the one answering emails with a tight stomach. The one who decides how much they will tolerate. The one who chooses whether to speak up or stay quiet one more time. That is identity in motion.

This is why understanding something does not automatically lead to change.

Insight lives in the mind, but behavior lives in the body. And when pressure shows up, the nervous system does not consult with what you *know*, it defaults to what it recognizes as safe.

In moments of stress, urgency, or emotional threat, your system reaches for familiarity. The body is not optimized for growth; it is optimized for survival. So, unless that moment gets interrupted, the same version of you keeps deciding — even when you genuinely want something different.

Change begins the moment you stop letting the past choose for you.

Familiar Feels Safer Than Better

We must stop thinking that we are regressing when we repeat patterns.

You are not. You are just going back to what feels familiar and safe.

Your nervous system does not operate on happiness it operates on **predictability.** It does this because predictability is comfortable. And as humans we love comfortability. The human brain will do anything in its power to make you comfortable in your environment.

When things get easier, your body does not trust it. Peace feels suspicious when you are wired for survival.

This is where people get stuck. They try to change their actions without changing their core identity. They want new outcomes while still moving like the same person.

But identity does not update through declarations. It updates through **evidence.**

Evidence looks like:

- Doing the thing you usually avoid
- Stopping something you normally tolerate

- Letting yourself be seen a little more
- Not abandoning yourself when discomfort shows up.

Small things.

But powerful.

Because every time you act differently, your body quietly takes notes.

Oh. We do this now.

And slowly, the response you get changes too.

Identity Is Memory

Your identity is who you trust yourself to be. Identity is not a label. It is a *relationship* you have with yourself.

Do you trust yourself to rest?

To receive?

To say no and not explain it?

To want more without apologizing?

Or do you still move like: You have to earn ease? You have to brace for disappointment? Like you shouldn't get too comfortable? Or like something will drop if you loosen your grip?

That is old programming.

And life listens to memory more than motivation. Which means if you want different outcomes, you have to give your body different evidence.

The Moment Everything Starts to Shift

There comes a time when you realize that you are not fighting as hard. You are not explaining yourself as much. You're not rushing every decision or waiting for permission to feel okay.

Your identity is catching up.

Life does not change because you want it to. It changes when your actions stop contradicting your intentions. When choices, boundaries, and expectations align, movement follows.

You don't need to reinvent yourself or become fearless, healed, or perfect. You only need to practice acting in slightly closer alignment with who you actually are.

Small shifts accumulate.

This is how my life changed.

Insight Without Evidence

We as humans, get frustrated because conscious thinking feels like work, and we are taught that work should lead to some kind of results. We are taught that if we understand what we are doing and why, things should change. So, when they don't, most people assume that they are the problem, and they do not consider the approach.

I had to learn this the hard way: you cannot think your way into a new life. Thinking happens at the same level as the patterns you are trying to change.

Most of what runs your life, how you react, what you avoid, what you repeat, are not stored in logic. It lives deeper than that in the body. It lives in the nervous system. Those patterns are built through experience, not common sense. So, when you try to think your way out of them, you are asking your mind to override something that your body learned through repetition and protection.

When that does not work, people normally double down. They go harder, analyze longer. And when nothing changes, the frustration turns inward. You start believing you are broken, lazy, or incapable of change.

But the truth is simpler than that. Knowing is different from doing. A new life does not come from better thoughts alone. It comes from doing things differently, over, and over, until it starts to feel normal. That's what actually shifts patterns.

Thinking can open the door, but living differently is what walks you through it.

Once I understood that, I stopped being mad and frustrated all the time. Not because changing got easier, but because I stopped trying to change at the wrong level.

You don't decide who you are once. You must constantly prove it to yourself through repetition and pace yourself.

Loyalty to Survival

Here is the part people don't like to talk about: an outdated identity doesn't just limit success. It limits pleasure, ease, joy, and your ability to receive.

You can have opportunities right in front of you and still miss them.

You can have love offered to you and still stay guarded.

You can have money come in and still feel unstable.

Not because you are ungrateful or negative, but because internally you're still moving like things could fall apart at any moment. That expectation shapes your choices. And choices shape outcomes.

It is not about thoughts or attitude. It is loyalty to what once kept you safe.

The moment things start to change is when identity begins to shift. It is when you don't abandon yourself. It is when you say no without explaining, when you can feel uncomfortable without panicking, when you can want more without talking yourself out of it, and when you can rest without justifying it. Something clicks, not in your head but in your body: *I am allowed to be here like this.* That moment matters more than any affirmation because it's evidence. And evidence is how identity updates the system.

Once your identity begins to shift, things start moving faster.

That is when people say,

"Things just started flowing."

They did not.

You stopped getting in your own way.

Identity is not who you were. It is who you're practicing being right now.

You are not trying to transform. You are giving an outdated version of yourself permission to retire.

And that does not happen by thinking differently. It happens by acting differently—over and over—until your system accepts it.

Those actions become patterns. Patterns become standards. And standards shape everything that comes next.

Daily Practice: Identity in Real Time (5–10 minutes)

1. **Notice the moment (today)**

Catch yourself in a familiar reaction:

Pay attention. Are you overthinking? Rushing? People-pleasing? Self-silencing?

2. **Ask one question**

Who do I usually become here?

Then ask:

Who am I practicing being now?

3. **Act small but true**

Choose the smallest action that aligns with the upgraded identity.

Not dramatic.

Just honest.

4. **Let it register**

Notice how your body responds.

This is how identity rewires — not in theory, but in life.

Daily Practice: Identity in Motion (5–10 minutes)

1. **Catch yourself (2 minutes)**

Notice one moment today where you did what you *always*

do.

Pause.

2. **Choose differently (real time)**
   Ask:

   What would the version of me am I becoming do here?

   Then do the smallest version of that.

3. **Let it land (1 minute)**

   Notice how your body feels afterward.

CHAPTER 7

STANDARDS

What You Allow Decides What Stays

Knowing Is not Choosing

Many people reach a point where they understand themselves. They can see the patterns. They know why they react the way they do and where it comes from. And still, nothing really changes.

Not because they do not care or aren't trying, but because insight alone doesn't stop a pattern. Life does not respond to what you understand. It responds to what you allow.

Adaption, Not Acceptance

A huge part of our lives is shaped by what we quietly tolerate.

If you put up with something you do not like long enough, your nervous system stops flagging it. It stops feeling urgent. It stops feeling wrong. It just starts to feel normal.

Normal is different from healthy. Normal is what is familiar.

At first, it's something small. A sharp comment. A tone that feels off. An apology that doesn't quite land. You notice it, then give a reason for why it happened. "They were stressed." "I'm being sensitive." "It's not that serious."

Then it happens again. And again.

Over time, your body adjusts. What once felt alarming starts to feel expected. You do not stay in alignment because things are safe — you stay alert because you have learned what to expect. The nervous system stops asking, *Is this okay?* and starts asking, *How do I get through this?*

That is how tolerance becomes natural.

In unhealthy or abusive relationships, this shift is not sudden. It is gradual. You accommodate. You get quieter. You do less to keep the peace. Eventually, what would have once felt unacceptable starts to feel like "just how things are."

What we tolerate does not stay in the outside world. No, it becomes our internal teacher. Teaching us what to expect, what to put up with, and what not to question. That is why leaving or setting boundaries later can feel disorienting. You are not just changing a relationship. You are retraining your reality on what safety feels like in your body.

Once you see how tolerance trains the nervous system, the next question becomes obvious: why doesn't awareness alone break the pattern? Because awareness without boundaries just means you understand why you're accepting what you shouldn't.

Healing is internal. Standards are the external shift. And without both, nothing really changes.

I remember the moment I recognized the disconnect. I was

completely calm in a situation that used to break me down. I knew what was happening. I could explain the whole pattern. And I couldn't bring myself to feel upset.

But I was still there. Still accepting it.

That is when I understood.

Healing changed how I felt. But it did not change what I was willing to tolerate. My awareness had grown, but my life looked the exact same way.

You can understand everything and still accept anything. That is not progress. That is just self-aware settling.

Consistency Over Confrontation

Standards are not about confrontation. They are about consistency.

A standard simply says: *this is what I can live with.*

It is information.

There is a story I heard years ago that stayed with me because it was not a dramatic story. It was actually very ordinary. And that reason alone is what made it so uncomfortable.

There was a woman who had been seeing the same therapist for years. Smart. Self-aware. Doing the work. She understood her patterns, could name her wounds, and knew exactly why she chose the relationships she did.

But her life was not changing.

One day, her therapist asked a question that had nothing to do with her childhood or her thinking.

"What kind of towels do you use?"

She laughed.

"Old ones. They still work."

The therapist asked:

"What about your sheets?"

She replied:

"Whatever is the cheapest."

The therapist then asked:

"How about your car?"

She replied:

"Messy, but manageable."

Lastly, she was asked:

"Well how do you feel about your apartment?"

She replied:

"Fine. Not bad. Just what was available."

Her therapist did not analyze anything. She did not explain it. She did not diagnose her. She just said simply,

"You treat your life like it's temporary."

That landed harder than anything else.

Because it was true.

She realized she lived like someone waiting. Waiting to earn better. Waiting to deserve more. Waiting for life to really start.

Nothing in her daily environment reflected care—only function.

When the woman got home, she tried something small.

She threw out the towels that she had been using since college. She went out and bought brand new ones. Not fancy or expensive towels. Just intentional ones that felt good. She purchased sheets that she actually liked touching, a trash can that closed properly and a chair that she didn't rush to get out of.

She did not announce it or post about it.

But something changed.

First, something shifted in her body. She moved slower at home. She stopped rushing to leave out. She rested without guilt.

A few months later, she left a relationship she had been making excuses about for years. Not because of a fight or a relationship altering moment. She just could not tolerate it anymore and nothing about the relationship changed. She changed.

Her standards had caught up to her awareness.

The lesson is so easy to miss.

Life does not change when you understand yourself. It changes when your standards stop matching an obsolete version of you. And standards are not about being demanding—they are about letting go of what you no longer agree with.

The Quiet Yes

Society talks about selling your soul like it is dramatic or rare. In real life, it usually looks like self-betrayal.

Self-betrayal is not necessarily loud, and it doesn't happen in big moments.

It happens quietly.

It happens when:

- you say yes when your body says no.
- you explain yourself when you do not need to
- you tolerate something you have already outgrown.
- you minimize what you feel to keep the peace.

Here is a simple exercise.

Stop for a minute and think about the last day or two. Ask yourself:

- Where did I say yes when I wanted to say no?
- Where did I stay quiet to keep things easy?
- Where did I minimize something that didn't sit right?

Then ask:

What did I gain by doing that?

(Relief? Less tension? Avoiding a conversation?)

And finally:

What did it cost me?

You do not need to fix anything yet. Just notice the trade off when it happened.

Self-betrayal is subtle. It is choosing what feels safest in the moment. Once you see it, you can stop it. Each time, it feels small. But repetition is how momentum builds.

Self-betrayal stops when awareness turns into choice. Each time you choose alignment over comfort, you send a different signal. Over time, those signals build momentum, and life stops requiring you to disappear in order to function.

Why Raising Your Standards Feel Uncomfortable at First

Raising your standards often feels uncomfortable at first because it registers as loss, not empowerment. You are not gaining something instantly; you are letting go of what used to make things predictable. And for a nervous system that learned safety through accommodation, predictability mattered more than comfort ever did.

When you stop accommodating, your body reacts first. The urge to explain, soften, or take it back hits immediately. Not because the standard is wrong but because it is new programming. Your system is trying to restore equilibrium.

This is where people retreat and begin to go back to their old ways. They feel uncomfortable and think they did something wrong. But discomfort is not a warning. It is an adjustment. Your body is learning a new baseline.

Evidence Changes Reality

Identity does not change through declarations. It updates through evidence and standards are how that evidence is created.

Every time you do not rush to explain, or override yourself, or when you no longer accept what no longer fits, something registers, physically. Your system begins to notice that a familiar outcome did not happen. It notices that you did not collapse, apologize, or lose connection just because you held a line.

This is how patterns begin to break form. Not because a new story was told, but because the body experienced something different and survived it.

It can be as small as saying no without a reason and sitting through the discomfort. Or not replying immediately. Or choosing rest without justifying it. The moment passes. Nothing that is meant to stay falls apart. And your nervous system quietly takes note.

Expectations adjust. Old predictions soften. Reality starts responding to a different signal.

There is no announcement. No identity overhaul. Just an internal update that sounds like:

Oh. We don't do that anymore.

As that evidence repeats, how you show up in life stops being theoretical. It becomes lived.

Life Responds to Standards, Not Intentions

Life will not respond to what you hope will change. It will respond to what consistently stays in place. Repetition, not intention, is what sets the tone. If something keeps happening to you, do not take it isn't a personal failure use it as information about what's being allowed to continue in your life.

Allowance is not always conscious. It shows up in what you keep answering, what you keep excusing, what you keep adapting around. The system reads consistency as consent.

When standards shift, patterns follow. Not because you forced a change, but because the signal changed. Old dynamics lose traction. New responses start to take hold. It does not happen overnight, but it becomes hard to miss.

This Is the Turning Point

Up until now, this book has helped you understand yourself. This chapter is where understanding becomes leverage.

You are not being asked to try harder. You are being asked to get clearer. And clarity changes how life meets you. One of my favorite sayings is simple: clarity in the vision accelerates the goal.

Daily Practice: Noticing Tolerance (5–10 minutes)

Today, notice one thing you usually excuse, minimize, or push through.

Ask yourself:

- What does this cost me?
- Why have I been allowing it?
- What would honoring myself look like here?

You do not have to act yet.

Just notice. Standards begin with awareness and solidify through repetition.

CHAPTER 8
STEPS

Language, Repetition, and Reality

Once I understood how much my body mattered, something else became impossible to ignore.

The way I talked to myself.

Not the words I posted.

Not the affirmations I tried to remember.

The quiet, constant language underneath everything.

The comments in my head.

The tone I used with myself when no one was listening.

The stories I repeated without realizing they were stories

I started noticing it in ordinary moments. I would misplace something and immediately think, *you always do this.* I would feel a little tired and hear, *you're falling behind again. And,* if something went smoothly, my mind would already be scanning for what might go wrong next. No big spiral. Just a steady, background narrator that assumed friction, difficulty, and eventual disappointment was on the way.

What stood out was not how harsh it was — it was how unquestioned it felt. I did not argue with those thoughts. I did not even notice them most of the time. The thoughts felt factual. Like commentary instead of judgment. And that is when I realized how powerful they were. This was the voice setting the conditions for how I moved throughout my day. How much effort I expected things to take. How much grace I gave myself. How much space that I believed I was allowed to occupy.

I was not speaking to myself like someone who expected support or even wanted it. I was speaking to myself like someone who expected resistance. And then I wondered why life felt heavy.

My language wasn't just something I was using. It was something I was living. It was shaping what I noticed, what I prepared for, and what I believed was possible before anything even happened.

And once I could hear it, I could not unhear it.

The First Sentence

When something goes wrong, most people do not pause to think, they start telling themselves stories.

There is always a first sentence:

- "Here we go again."
- "I can't deal with this."
- "This always happens."

These sentences do not describe the actual moment. They *decide* how your body manages it. The nervous system responds to tone, not logic; so, if the first sentence sounds urgent, critical, or final, the body prepares for a threat even if the situation is not threatening.

Language works before logic does. Long before a thought becomes a belief, it becomes a tone, something the body takes in and reacts to. The language you live with shapes your internal state, and that state quietly influences the experiences you allow, attract, or avoid. Language is not just expression. It is direction.

Before you act, before you decide, before you can change anything on the outside, there is always a sentence that runs through your mind. That sentence sets the tone for your nervous system, narrows, or widens your options, and determines whether you respond or react.

This chapter is about learning how to catch that sentence and choose a better first move.

Every time you tell yourself:

- "This is always hard."
- "I already know how this will go."
- "I can't deal with this right now."
- "That's just how I am."

Know that this is not venting, this is programming in action.

Believability Over Positivity

People get frustrated with positive thinking because they are trying to convince themselves of something they do not actually believe. We try to flip the script and tell ourselves; *I am confident. I am happy. I am healed.* But something inside of us resists.

That resistance is not negativity. It is honesty.

Your body knows when you are lying to yourself. The goal is not to sound positive. The goal is to sound safe enough to keep going.

When your words and actions do not match, you end up running in circles. You can say whatever you want aloud, but your internal voice is still working underneath it all.

That does not mean language is not powerful. It means it must be believable.

Here's the loop that keeps running, whether you notice it or not:

Language → nervous system → behavior → results

Results → reinforce language → repeat.

If what you are getting out of life does not change, it's not because you didn't try hard enough.

It's because the first signal never changed. Instead of trying to tell yourself *"I'm confident"* or *"I'm healed,"* make a smaller shift. Ground your words in reality. This sounds more like, *this is what's happening*, or *I don't know yet.* No reassurance. No conclusion. Just enough neutrality that your body does not escalate the moment.

That is the point. Neutral language is not meant to feel good. It is meant to stop the spiral. It keeps you from deciding too much, too fast, and that is often enough to change what happens next.

Language Keeps the Loop Alive

Most people do not realize they are living inside a loop. A loop about who they are. What is possible for them. What always happens. What's "realistic." And over time, those ideas stop feeling like thoughts and start feeling like facts.

Once a story has momentum, life keeps confirming it; not because the story is true, but because you think it is. You expect certain outcomes, prepare for them, and subtly move in ways that make them more likely. It's not on purpose it is done automatically. The loop feeds itself.

This is why arguing with the story rarely works. You can logic your way through it, explain why it is not accurate, even try to prove the story wrong — and still live it. Because the loop is not sustained by evidence. The loop is sustained by repetition, the language you use internally and by the energy you live inside.

Loops stay alive through what you keep saying to yourself when things happen — especially when you are tired, unsure, or under pressure. When the language stays the same, the story stays the same. When the language shifts, even slightly, the loop begins to break.

You do not exit a loop overnight just like you did not get into it overnight.

You exit it by stopping the repetition. One sentence at a time.

Why Self-Talk Shapes Biology

The way you talk to yourself is not just psychological. It is physiological.

Your brain and nervous system do not respond to meaning, they respond to signals. Tone matters more than logic. So, when your inner language is critical, urgent, or threatening, your brain interprets it as danger. The threat system activates, and your body shifts into protection mode.

In that state:

- focus narrows.
- creativity drops.
- risk-taking decreases
- decision-making becomes reactive.

Your body is not preparing to grow. It is preparing to survive.

That is why intelligent, motivated people still repeat the same patterns. It has nothing to do with capability or willpower. It is a stress signal. Repeated thoughts strengthen neural pathways. What you rehearse becomes automatic. What becomes automatic turns into behavior.

So, when your inner dialogue sounds like:

- "Don't mess this up."
- "I can't afford to fail."
- "I always screw this up."

Your system is not being motivated. It is being warned.

And when the body feels warned, it prioritizes:

- avoidance over initiative

- familiarity over improvement
- short-term relief over long-term growth

Not because you lack ambition, your system is just doing exactly what it was designed to do.

This is why change does not come from pushing harder or thinking more positively. When urgency is running the system, your body will always choose what feels safest, not what sounds best on paper. You can want more and still pull back from it. You can see the opportunity and still hesitate. Not because you lack courage or clarity, but because your internal language is signaling threat instead of capacity.

Lowering that signal does not mean losing your drive. It means removing unnecessary pressure so different options can register. When the tone inside softens, the range of choices widens. You do not become a different person. You become less reactive. And from there, movement stops being forced and starts being possible.

Regulation Through Words

Effective self-talk does not sound like hype.

It sounds something your soul and body actually believe.

It does not push. It does not demand. It does not rush the outcome. It gives the nervous system enough stability to stay present with what is happening instead of bracing against it.

So instead of,

"I have to get this right,"

the language shifts to something truer and less loaded:

"I can take this one step at a time."

Instead of,

"This can't fail,"

it becomes:

"I can manage the outcome either way."

Nothing about this is motivational. It is practical. These kinds of statements do not try to control the future — they reduce pressure in the present. And when pressure drops, attention widens. Options reappear. The part of the brain responsible for planning, creativity, and follow-through becomes available again.

That is the real mechanism. Change does not happen because you told yourself a better story. It happens because your body stopped resisting the moment long enough for you to respond instead of reacting.

How I Changed My Own Language

Changing the way that I spoke to myself and others was not easy. Even with me thinking I was an overtly positive person, the more I paid attention to the thoughts running fast in my head, I realized that the thoughts were not necessarily negative, they were just extremely underwhelming. So, I started small. I did not try to sound confident or positive. I tried to sound as **accurate as possible**. When thoughts would pop up in my head, I would rush to replace the wording.

Instead of saying:

"I'm stuck."

I said:

"I'm in a transition."

Instead of:

"I can't manage this."

I said:

"God has this."

Those small shifts mattered not only because they were inspirational but because my body believed them. And when my body believed them, my behavior followed.

From Thought to Action

Good language does not float above your life. It walks you through it. It helps you pause instead of spiral, choose instead of reacting, and stay present instead of catastrophizing.

Over time, the correct language changes how you see yourself and that changes how you move.

You do not need to think better. You need to rehearse better. Change does not happen when things are calm. It happens when you are tired. When you are disappointed. When something does not go as planned.

That is when your language is actively shaping your reality.

That is when your words matter most.

That's when repetition becomes your life.

Daily Practice: Language Rehearsal

You do not need better thoughts. You need a better first sentence.

1. **Catch one phrase**

Notice one thing you say to yourself automatically when something feels uncomfortable.

2. **Replace it with something believable**

Not overly positive — just slightly more supportive.

Example:

- From: “This is too much.”
- To: “This is a lot, and I can take it step by step.”

3. **Repeat on purpose (same day)**

Use the new phrase every time the old one tries to come back.

No force. Just consistency.

That is how language retrains reality.

CHAPTER 9

STAY

Conscious Creation in a Fast World

There has always been power in intention and creation.

Long before technology, long before psychology, long before we had language for nervous systems or behavioral patterns, people understood a simple truth: what you return your attention to, consistently and with feeling, begins to shape your experience of life.

They did not explain it in clinical terms. They lived it.

They called it prayer — not as a request, but as orientation.

They called it meditation — not as escape, but as focus.

They called it alignment with God, Spirit, or divine law — not as belief, but as relationship.

Different words. Same function.

What mattered was not the label. It was the relationship, the direction, and the willingness to stay with something long enough for it to take root. Intention was not about wanting something badly. It was about choosing where your attention goes, over and over again, even when there is no evidence that the circumstances had changed yet.

That part that has not changed.

Life does not respond to wishes or passing thoughts. It responds to what you consistently direct yourself toward — with your focus, your choices, and your follow-through. Conscious direction has always been the mechanism. We have just learned new language for how it works.

And when your intention is steady, your life tends to organize itself around what you focus on; good or bad.

Seeing the Pattern

When I first started meditating, I was not trying to manifest anything.

I was not sitting there trying to visualize cars, money, or some perfect future version of myself. I was honestly just trying to quiet my mind. I needed a break from my own thoughts.

At first, nothing dramatic happened.

My mind wandered. I questioned if I was "doing it right."

But I kept coming back to it, not every day at first, just consistently enough to notice something.

My thoughts slowed down.

And when they slowed down, I started to notice what I was thinking about *all the time* without realizing it.

Not affirmations, not goals, but worries about conversations I had not had yet, outcomes I was preparing for and things I assumed would go wrong.

Here is what surprised me.

As my mind got quieter, I began to see my life more clearly.

Not in a magical way, in a practical way. I began to pay attention to the patterns and omens that were showing up.

The things that kept turning over in my head started showing up in my environment.

The conversations I rehearsed internally seemed to happen aloud. The situations I expected, I kept walking into them.

At first, it felt uncanny. I thought maybe it's just a coincidence. Then it felt obvious.

Meditation did not make my thoughts more powerful.

Meditation made my thoughts more **visible**.

And once I made the connection, I couldn't unsee it.

I was not attracting from intention.

I was attracting from **attention**.

Whatever had my attention, whether it be emotionally, mentally, physically, or financially; it was shaping how I moved, what I noticed, and what I responded to.

Meditation did not change my life overnight.

It changed *me* just enough for me to start to respond to life differently.

I spoke differently.

I listened more.

And because of that, different things had room to find me.

That is when I understood something important:

Stillness does not create things, being still reveals what is already in the process of being created.

And once you see that, you are no longer creating blindly, you become a conscious participator.

Slowing down did not make my thoughts louder; it made me understand that I am responsible for them.

Urgency Breaks Presence

The opposite of being still is not distraction. It is the state of urgency.

Urgency is the impulse to fix, explain, optimize, or escape a moment before it finishes. It often wears productive disguises — planning, managing things, staying busy — but underneath is the same message: *this moment is not safe to be in.*

When urgency takes over, the state of being present falls apart. Your body tightens, your mind speeds up and your attention narrows. And instead of responding to what is actually happening, you move to end the feeling as soon as possible.

This is why urgency feels powerful in the moment. It creates motion. But it is reactive motion. Its movement driven by needing relief, not direction.

Being still does not mean doing nothing. It means letting one moment complete before acting on it. It is not reaching for your phone immediately. Not rushing to name what you feel. Not turning uncertainty into a plan just to regain a sense of control.

Stillness is staying long enough to feel what is going on without needing to change it first.

That pause is where choice returns. And when choice returns, power does too.

Urgent action requires decisive action. It moves fast. It meets the discomfort first. The goal is not accuracy, it is relief. Something getting said, a need being met, something getting decided. The anxiety ends, even if the situation does not improve.

Intentional action is quieter. It waits for the moment to settle before moving. It does not rush to resolve the feeling. It lets information surface. The action comes from clarity, not pressure. It may look slower, but it creates fewer corrections later.

The difference is not motivation. It is timing.

I noticed this in myself in small moments. A message would come in and my body would instantly get anxious. My first impulse was to respond immediately — to explain, clarify, fix the energy before it turned into something worse. When I followed that impulse, I usually said too much or committed too quickly. Not because it was what I wanted— but because I wanted the pressure gone.

The times I did not rush, something else happened. The urge passed. The message did not mean what I thought it did. Or it meant something I did not need to manage right then. Waiting did not make me lose control. It gave it back.

That is the difference urgency hides. It makes action feel necessary when it is just premature.

And once you see that, stillness stops feeling passive. It feels precise.

Direction, Not Request

Prayer is not begging or bargaining. It is direction.

A lot of people are taught that prayer is asking, asking for help, relief, protection, or for something outside of them to change. And when prayer is framed that way, it can feel passive, like you are waiting for permission or intervention. But that's not how prayer has functioned historically, and it is not how it actually works in practice.

At its core, prayer is orientation. It is how you decide what you are turning toward internally. It is a way of setting a direction before your circumstances shift; not by forcing change, but by changing how you meet what's already here.

Prayer turns your attention, your posture, and your internal tone towards what you want to live. Towards steadiness instead of panic. Towards trust instead of urgency. Towards presence instead of resistance. It is less about asking for a different outcome and more about choosing the perspective you bring into the outcome that's unfolding.

That is why prayer feels different depending on where it comes from. When it is rooted in fear, it feels uneasy, urgent, and repetitive — like trying to convince something to go your way. When it is rooted in trust, it feels quieter. More settled. Less like control and more like alignment.

True prayer is not about convincing God to act. It is about aligning yourself with what you're asking to receive. It is about becoming someone who can hold the thing you're praying for — emotionally, mentally, and physically.

Prayer does not always change what happens next. But it

consistently changes how you show up when it does. And that shift in presence, over time, is often what changes everything.

Stillness as Information

If prayer is speaking, meditation is listening.

Not listening for voices — listening for clarity and information. Listening for what's underneath the noise, the voice that is usually running the show. It allows the body to settle. The breath evens out. The urgency drops. Space opens between what happening and how you choosing to respond to it.

Being still is not about stopping your thoughts or escaping your life. It is about seeing what is already there without immediately reacting to it. It is a return to yourself — not as a concept, but as a felt state.

You do not meditate to escape your life. You meditate to show up for it more clearly.

A few minutes of stillness can recalibrate how you move through the rest of your day.

Participation Changes Outcome

Intention is where prayer and practice meet. It is not passive. It is an action-based work.

An intention is not just what you ask for. It is how you choose to move through what is already happening. It sets the tone before the moment tests you.

An intention says:

- This is the energy I am carrying today.

- This is how I am choosing to respond when things don't go smoothly.
- This is who I am practicing being, even when it's uncomfortable.

Intentions do not control outcomes. They do not guarantee results. What they do is shape participation. They determine how present you are, how reactive you are, and what version of yourself shows up when it counts.

And participation is where change happens. Not all at once. Not dramatically. But consistently enough that life starts meeting you differently.

The World Is Faster — The Law Is the Same

We live in a time where everything moves quickly. Information spreads instantly. Ideas multiply. Tools amplify thought and action in real time. But speed does not change spiritual law. It magnifies it.

What's unfocused scatters faster.

What's intentional gains momentum quicker.

What's unconscious drains energy more rapidly.

In a slower world, you could move without much awareness and still stay upright. In this new world, every signal you send gets amplified. Attention leaks cost more, reactivity compounds and misalignments show up faster.

This is why inner clarity matters more than ever. Not as a concept, but as a stabilizer. It determines what you give energy to, what you ignore, and what you reinforce through repetition.

In a fast world, clarity is not optional. It is a protective measure.

Tools Respond to the Clarity You Bring

Modern tools, including technology, do not create power. They reflect it.

They respond to the questions you ask, the intention behind your actions, and the steadiness of your emotional state. Technology does not decide direction — it follows it. A scattered mind gets scattered results. A clear heart produces clear direction. Not because the tool is intuitive, but because it magnifies whatever signal it has been given.

That is why technology cannot replace prayer, meditation, or discernment or doing the challenging work. Those practices stabilize the signal. They determine what you are actually bringing to the table, is it urgency or clarity, a reaction or intention. Technology amplifies whatever you give it. When your inner world is unfocused, the output is noisy. When your inner state is steady, the output becomes precise.

The tool is not the source.

You are.

The responsibility of this era is not to reject progress. It is to stay anchored. Anchored in your body. Anchored in your values. Anchored in your relationship with God, Spirit, or inner truth.

When you start your day grounded, the world feels less invasive. When you pause before reacting, you remain sovereign. When you move with intention, speed does not erase depth.

Conscious creation is not about controlling life.

It's about collaborating with it deliberately.

How to Re-Ground

Re-grounding is not about fixing your mood or calming down perfectly. It is about returning to your body and your point of choice.

Start simple.

First, **pause movement**. Not forever. Just long enough to stop adding momentum. Sit, stand, or place both feet on the floor. Let the moment finish before you decide what comes next.

Second, **scan your body**. Feel something concrete — your feet, your hands, your breath moving in and out. You are not trying to relax. You are reminding your system where you are.

Third, **narrow your focus**. Ask one neutral question:

What is actually happening right now?

Not what might happen. Not what it means. Just what is real in this moment.

Fourth, **remove urgency from language**. Drop words like *now, always, never.* Replace them with something factual:

This is what's in front of me.

That is enough to steady the signal.

Finally, **choose one small next action**. Not a whole plan. Not a solution. Just the next right-sized move. Re-grounding works when action follows clarity — not pressure.

This does not take long. A minute is enough. Sometimes less.

You do not need to re-ground to escape life. You re-ground so you can meet life without losing yourself in the process.

And the more often you do this, the faster your system remembers the way back.

Daily Practice: Prayer, Stillness, and Intention

If your practice doesn't change how you pause, it isn't ingrained yet.

1. **Opening Prayer (1–2 minutes)**

    Speak aloud or silently:

"Today, I align my thoughts, actions, and energy with what is meant for me."

Let it land.

2. **Stillness (2–3 minutes)**
    Sit quietly.

    Breathe naturally.

    Notice your body.

No forcing. Just presence.

3. **Set One Intention (1 minute)**
    Complete the sentence:

"Today, I choose to move with ___."

Peace.

Clarity.

Trust.

Courage.

4. **Live It Once (same day)**

   Let that intention guide **one choice** today.

That is conscious creation.

CHAPTER 10

PRACTICE

Making Alignment Familiar

At some point, understanding stops being enough.

You can know all the concepts.

You can see the patterns clearly.

You can even feel hopeful again.

And still — you must practice.

Not imagine.

Not plan.

Practice.

This is where most people fall short. Not because they do not care, but because they expect insight to carry them the rest of the way. They believe once something *clicks*, life should follow. When it doesn't, they think they did something wrong.

Change doesn't announce itself. It shows up quietly,

through repetition. Through choosing the same aligned response again tomorrow. And the day after that. Even when it feels uneventful. Even when no one sees it. Even when it does not feel like progress yet.

Real change rarely feels powerful at first. It feels regular. Slightly inconvenient. Almost boring. This is how you know it's real because it's not fueled by adrenaline or inspiration. It is sustained by consistency.

Practice is where understanding becomes embodied. It is where intention turns into behavior. It is how something new stops being an idea and starts becoming your default.

The part most people underestimate is the part that actually lasts.

The Life You Want Is a journey, not a Destination.

Most people treat the life they want like a finish line.

But life does not work that way.

You do not arrive at the life you want — you practice it into existence. How you move today is teaching your system what to expect tomorrow.

Opportunity lives here.

There is no moment where you finally get it all right and never struggle again. No finish line where you are permanently healed, confident, or certain. What exists instead is repetition.

How you show up — today.

How you speak to yourself.

How you treat your body.

How you respond when things do not go as planned.

How you come back to yourself when you lose your footing.

Progress is not about perfection

It's about participation.

And participation is a life skill that turns effort into a life that feels lived.

Practice Before Proof

Waiting keeps people stuck because waiting often feels responsible. Practicing feels risky.

Waiting says: *I will live fully when things are settled.*

Practicing says: *I'm willing to live aligned before they are.*

Most people wait for proof before they change how they move. But proof does not come first. It comes after practice. This is why so many people feel like they are "almost there" for years. They are waiting for life to shift before they do.

But its movement that builds trust.

The Bible is clear on this principle: faith does not wait for evidence. It moves before confirmation. Scripture does not describe faith as believing harder. It describes faith as alignment. It is living as if what you trust is already true, even when the outcome isn't visible yet.

The pattern repeats repeatedly:

- Abraham moves without knowing where he is going.
- Moses steps forward before the sea parts.

- Peter steps out of the boat before he knows he can stand.

Faith is never passive.

It is participatory.

In real life, which looks like acting with integrity before the reward, choosing trust before reassurance, and moving in the direction you believe is right — even when certainty hasn't arrived yet.

Faith does not mean pretending everything is okay. It means practicing trust long enough for your body, your mind, and your actions to agree.

Sight comes later.

Faith always leads.

This happened before I was deep in any spiritual practice. I was not manifesting. I was not affirming. I was just trying to get through what was in front of me.

My kids needed things. Real things. Clothes. Supplies. Stability. I needed a car. I needed to get to California. When I finally added it up, it was about ten thousand dollars. Not a goal — a gap.

I did not know where it was supposed to come from. I was not calm about it. I was tired.

That day, my grandmother took me to Family Dollar to get detergent so I could wash clothes. Just basics. I went to the ATM to pull out cash. Nothing about the moment felt special. No expectation. No prayer I remember saying out loud. Just doing what needed to be done.

As I walked away from the machine, something nudged me

to check my phone. No urgency. Just a pull. I opened my mobile banking app.

There it was.

$9,873.

I stared at the screen. Refreshed it. Looked again. I had no explanation for it. No deposit I was expecting. No check I remembered. Nothing pending. It was just... there.

I did not scream. I did not fall to my knees. I stood in the parking lot and felt something release in my chest — not excitement, relief. Like my body finally unclenched from something it had been holding.

Later, I would understand this moment differently. But at the time, all I knew was this: I had stopped trying to force the next step. I was doing what was in front of me. I had not waited to feel secure before moving. I moved — and security showed up.

The proof did not come because I demanded it.

It came after I stopped gripping the moment.

I did not have language for it then.

But that was practice before proof.

And once you experience that kind of alignment — even once — you do not forget what's possible when you move without bargaining with fear.

Practice Is Where Identity, Attention, and Capacity Meet

By now, you have seen the pattern.

Identity shapes how you move.

Attention fuels what grows.

Capacity determines what you can hold.

Practice is where they come together.

Practicing the tools in this book is not about doing something big or dramatic. It is about repetition. Every small choice you make consistently becomes a vote for the life you are building.

Not life-altering decisions.

Regular ones.

How you start your morning.

How you speak when you are frustrated.

What you tolerate.

What you rest from.

What you return to

That is the work.

Awkward Comes First

Here is the part most people don't like.

You will not feel ready before you practice. You will feel slightly uncomfortable. A little exposed, you may even be unsure if it's working.

That is normal.

Practice always feels awkward before it feels natural. You do not wait to feel confident to practice confidence. You do not wait to feel calm to practice regulation. You do not wait to feel worthy to practice receiving.

You practice first.

The feeling follows.

Pressure vs. Trust

Forcing is loud.

Practice is quiet.

Forcing says, *I have to change everything now.*

Practice says, *I can do one thing differently today.*

Forcing creates pressure.

Practice builds trust.

Your system does not need to be shocked into change. It does not need intensity or urgency. It needs evidence — repeated experiences that show something new is safe.

That is how capacity expands.

That's how attention stabilizes.

That's how identity becomes lived.

Not all at once.

But unmistakably.

What I Mean by "Practice"

A practice is not something you graduate from. It is how life becomes livable. You do not wait for certainty, motivation, or proof before you move — you move with care, attention, and honesty, and let consistency do what intensity never could.

Over time, what once felt deliberate becomes natural, not because you forced change, but because you practiced a way of living that your body could trust.

When I say practice, I do not mean adding more to your plate. I mean pausing instead of pushing. Choosing rest without justification. Speaking honestly once instead of rehearsing silence. Closing the loop on one small promise to yourself. Practice is a lived experience, not something to be announced. And it compounds.

You know the practice is working when you no longer react as fast, when you do not spiral as deep, when you don't abandon yourself as quickly. That is progress. Not perfection.

Life does not suddenly become easy. You learn how to manage it better. And that steadiness changes outcomes.

You are Not Behind — You are Building.

If you take nothing else from this chapter, take this: you do not need to overhaul your life. You need to practice alignment in small ways, consistently.

That is how the life you want stops feeling distant and starts feeling familiar.

And familiar is what the nervous system allows to stay.

Daily Practice: Living It Before It is Finished

Today, choose **one small behavior** that matches the life you want.

Not tomorrow.

Not next week.

Today.

Ask:

If the life I want were already mine, how would I move right now?

Then do the smallest version of that.

Let it count.

That is how practice becomes reality.

CHAPTER 11
RECEIVE

Wealth, Love, and Capacity

I am almost certain you are not struggling with wanting more.

You are more likely struggling with receiving more.

Receiving money.

Receiving love.

Receiving help.

Receiving ease.

Receiving good things without immediately waiting for the cost

Almost no one talks about receiving. And when they do, it is usually oversimplified or mystified. People say things like, *"You just have to be open,"* or *"You have to believe your worthy."* But receiving is not a belief problem.

It is a capacity problem.

Wanting comes easily. Receiving requires stillness. It is not about holding onto something forever, and it's not about pushing it away as soon as it arrives. Receiving is something the nervous system can learn.

When something good happens, notice your first response — not your thoughts, but your body. Do you tighten up? Does your heart race? Do you feel the urge to give something back immediately, explain it, or prepare for what might go wrong?

That reaction is not random. It is conditioning. It shows you how much your body can hold in that moment.

There is a scene in **Next Friday** that most people laugh at and miss. Craig's aunt wins the lottery — real money, life-changing money. When the check arrives and she sees the amount, there is no joy. No relief. No celebration. Her body panics. She grabs her chest and collapses.

The joke is that the money killed her because the only time she saw that many zeros was on a scale. But the truth is was less comical: her system could not receive it.

She was built for survival — bills, pressure, holding things together. So, when something that good showed up, her body did not read it as a gift. It read it as danger.

Most people do not collapse like that. But they do something similar. They rush past the moment. They minimize it. They give it back. Or they brace for the worst before the good has a chance to settle.

Not because they do not want more — but because their body doesn't know how to hold more yet.

Receiving is not about deserving. It is about being able to stay present when something good arrives. Not explaining it away. Not justifying it. Not preparing for the fallout. Just allowing it to be there.

That, too, is a practice.

When Blessings Trigger Defense

For many of us, good things did not come without strings attached. Love came with responsibility. Money came with stress. Attention came with expectations. Help came with guilt.

So, the body learned:

Do not relax too much.

Do not get used to this.

Do not depend on it

Even when life improves, that mindset stays intact.

Not because you are pessimistic but because you are protective.

Good things feel uncomfortable when your nervous system is trained to survive. Comfort comes from staying long enough for your body to learn that ease does not equate to danger.

Getting comfortable with good things does not mean forcing gratitude or telling yourself to "enjoy it." That usually backfires. It means **letting your system acclimate slowly**, the same way it adapted to stress, but in reverse.

You start by:

- allowing good moments to last a few seconds longer
- noticing the urge to sabotage, rush, or downplay them.

- staying present instead of bracing for the drop

Comfort with good things grows through **exposure**, not belief.

You do not convince your body that safety is okay.

You show it that it is, repeatedly, in small ways.

And over time, what once felt uncomfortable starts to feel normal, not because you earned it, but because you finally taught your system what had to go and what could stay.

More Activates Safety

Something most people do not realize is that wealth and love activate the same response system in the body. When love deepens or money increases, real chemistry is released. Dopamine signals reward and importance. Oxytocin opens attachment and bonding. Together, they create intensity.

If the nervous system has not learned how to stay regulated while receiving, that intensity can tip into stress. Cortisol enters the picture. The body does not sort experiences into "good" or "bad." It asks one question: *Is this safe?* When the answer is unclear, the system tightens, rushes, or minimizes.

Not because the good thing is wrong — but because it is more than the body knows how to handle.

That is why people sabotage relationships, mishandle money, or feel anxious right when life improves. Receiving isn't a mindset issue. It is a nervous-system skill, built through repeated experiences of safety while something good is happening.

The same response shows up when:

- money increases
- love deepens.
- visibility grows.
- support becomes available.

All of those mean *more to hold.*

And if your system learned survival through self-reliance, receiving can feel threatening — even when it is wanted, even when it is needed. Not because you do not desire more, but because your body hasn't practiced staying present while more is available.

That is what this work trains.

Conditioning Not Character

For Many Women: Receiving Triggers Guilt

Many women are conditioned early to be considerate, self-sacrificing, emotionally available, and "easy to deal with." So, when something good arrives — money, support, rest, love — the internal response is not always relief. Sometimes it is guilt.

Thoughts like:

- *Did I earn this?*
- *Who am I burdening?*
- *I do not want to take too much.*

Receiving can feel like taking.

Ease can feel irresponsible.

Being supported can feel like weakness.

So instead of receiving fully, many women over-give to balance the scale. They minimize needs. They rush to reciprocate. Not because they do not want or need support, but because they learned to survive by being useful.

For Many Men: Receiving Triggers Threat

Men are often conditioned to equate worth with providing, solving, leading, and being needed. So, receiving can trigger something different — a threat to competence, a fear of dependency, a sense of losing position.

Thoughts like:

- *If I accept this, what does it say about me?*
- *I should be able to handle this on my own.*
- *I don't want to owe anyone.*

Instead of guilt, the response is often resistance. Instead of shrinking, it looks like control. Help is often rejected. Praise is deflected. Care feels uncomfortable.

Not because support is not wanted — but because safety was learned through self-sufficiency.

The Common Link

Underneath both patterns is the same truth: receiving challenges identity before it challenges worth.

For many women, receiving can challenge belonging.

For many men, receiving can challenge competence.

In both cases, the nervous system asks the same question:

Is it safe to let this in and still be who I am?

If the answer is unclear, the system tightens or shuts down. Lack of gratitude isn't the issue. Safety is.

Receiving Isn't Gendered — It's Regulated

No one needs to become "more masculine" or "more feminine" to receive. They need to feel safe doing so in their body.

Receiving becomes possible when:

- women no longer feel they must earn rest or love.
- men no longer feel they must carry everything alone.

Safety — not identity performance — is what allows abundance to stay.

When receiving is regulated:

- women stop apologizing for expansion.
- men stop isolating in strength.

And life stops being something you manage — and starts being something that meets you.

Receiving is not something you figure out once. It is something you practice in real time — moment by moment — as life offers you more than you're used to holding. Each time you stay present instead of shrinking, explaining, or bracing, your system learns that good things do not have to be dangerous. Over time, receiving stops feeling foreign and starts feeling natural. And when that happens, more does not feel overwhelming — it feels appropriate.

Strength as a Ceiling

There is a difference between being capable and being

guarded. Many strong people confuse the two.

They take pride in doing it alone. In not needing much. In being "low maintenance." In not asking. At first, that strength looks like freedom. Control. Competence.

But over time, it becomes a ceiling.

Not because independence is wrong, but because constant self-reliance leaves no room for support to land. Everything must pass through effort. Everything costs energy. Nothing is allowed to meet you halfway.

Receiving requires trust. Not blind trust — regulated trust. The kind that knows when to stay open without giving yourself away. When to accept help without losing yourself. When to let something in without bracing for the cost.

Strength stops being useful when it only protects you from needing anything. At that point, it is not capacity — it is armor. And armor may keep you safe, but it also keeps you alone.

Real strength is not ever needing support.

It is knowing when you no longer have to refuse it.

For a long time, when something good happened, I moved past it quickly.

A compliment got minimized.

An opportunity got questioned.

Support got repaid immediately.

Not consciously but automatically.

I did not want to owe anyone.

I did not want to depend on anyone.

I did not want to be disappointed.

So, I kept everything moving. I acknowledged the good just long enough not to seem ungrateful, then I redirected, deflected, or returned it. I told myself I was being responsible. Independent. Low maintenance. But underneath that level of efficiency was tension. A constant need to stay ahead of the moment before it could ask something of me.

That's when I realized I wasn't actually receiving — I was managing. Managing expectations. Managing exposure. Managing the risk of wanting too much. And life responds very differently to management than it does to openness.

Management keeps things contained. Predictable. Limited. Openness creates space. Not for chaos — but for support, connection, and ease to land without being immediately negotiated away.

And once I saw that difference, I could not unsee it.

That is how strength quietly became a ceiling for me. What looked like independence was actually guarding. What felt like capability was really control. I was not open to support — I was filtering it. And anything filtered never fully arrives. Strength kept me functional, but it also kept me contained. Once I saw that, receiving stopped feeling like weakness and started feeling like something I deserved. I gained the ability to let something enjoyable stay without needing to control it. And what a blessing that was.

Receiving Is a Skill

Understanding this changes everything: receiving isn't something you either can or can't do. It is a skill you practice.

You practice receiving when you say, "thank you" and stop there. When you let help actually help, when you enjoy a good moment without shrinking it. When you let yourself feel supported without planning your exit. These moments may look small, but they are not. They are teaching your system something important: *this is safe enough. I am allowed to have this.* And safety is what allows wealth and love to stay.

You Don't Have to Become Someone Else

You do not have to turn into a different person to receive more. You do not have to be softer, louder, or more confident than you are. You do not need a personality upgrade.

You just have to stop rushing past the good. Stop tightening when experiences are trying to expand. Stop proving you do not need it. Stop preparing for loss before anything has even happened.

Receiving does not require perfection. It requires your presence.

When Receiving Changes Your Life

You notice the shift quietly. You don't chase as hard. You do not second-guess as much. You rest without guilt.

Not because life is suddenly perfect — but because you are no longer blocking what is already being offered.

That is when wealth feels steadier.

That's when love feels safer.

That's when life starts meeting you halfway.

Receiving changes everything the moment you stop waiting for it to be taken away. That shift doesn't happen once. It happens daily. And that's where we go next.

Daily Practice: Practicing Receiving

You don't receive by proving you deserve something. You receive by not blocking it when it arrives.

Today, notice one moment when something good shows up.

A kind word.

A break.

A compliment.

A small win.

Instead of brushing past it, pause.

Take one breath and say:

"I can let this land."

That is enough.

That is how receiving grows.

CHAPTER 12
LIVE

Purpose Without Burnout

At some point, the goal stops being *more* and starts being a life you do not need to escape from. Not a perfect life. Not a constantly improving one. Just a life that feels livable — one where your body is not always tense, your mind isn't always racing, and your spirit isn't constantly being tested.

Living on purpose is not about effort or intensity. It is about sustainability. It is about choosing ways of working, healing, loving, and growing that don't require you to abandon yourself to keep going. Burnout does not come from caring too much — it comes from overriding your signals for too long.

When you can stay present — not replaying the past, not rehearsing the future — something shifts. Life stops feeling like a series of problems to solve or goals to chase and starts feeling like a series of choices you are actually inside of. You respond instead of reacting. You move with awareness instead of urgency.

There is also a difference between having knowledge and being able to live with it. Knowledge can inform you, but wisdom steadies you. Wisdom knows when to move and when to pause. When to stretch and when to rest. When understanding settles into the body, it changes your pace. It softens the need to prove, to rush, to overperform.

That is the part no one glamorizes. There is no highlight reel for living within your capacity. But it is the part that lasts. It is the part that keeps your life intact — not just productive, but whole.

Quiet Alignment

You can burn out chasing purpose when you believe it is supposed to look a certain way — big, visible, impressive, always meaningful. We are taught that if something is truly "purpose-driven," it should feel intense, consuming, or constantly productive. So, we push. We perform. We measure ourselves by how much impact we are making instead of how intact we feel while making it.

But purpose is not something you perform for an audience. It's something you practice quietly; in ways most people never see. It lives in how you pace yourself instead of rushing. In how you listen when your body asks for rest. In how you stop forcing outcomes just to prove you are on the right path.

Purpose shows up in the small, unglamorous decisions — choosing rest without guilt, saying no when something drains you, allowing your life to unfold at a pace you can actually sustain. That kind of purpose does not burn you out, because it does not require you to override yourself to keep going.

Purpose is not urgency.

It's alignment.

And alignment is what lets your life grow without costing

you your well-being.

Ignoring the Body

People do not burn out because they care too much. They burn out because they ignore themselves for too long. They push past signals. They override fatigue. They silence discomfort. They keep going even when something inside them is clearly saying, *slow down.*

That kind of effort costs more than it gives. It depletes instead of builds.

Living on purpose means learning when to move — and when to pause — without turning either into a problem. It is not about productivity or passivity. It is about responsiveness. Knowing when forward motion is aligned and when rest is the most honest choice you can make.

You Don't Need to Fix Your Whole Life

This is where I want to be very clear.

You don't need to overhaul your life to live it well. You don't need a new identity, a perfect routine, or constant clarity. You don't need to have everything figured out.

You need presence.

Presence when you choose.

Presence when you rest.

Presence when things feel messy or unfinished.

Purpose isn't found in control. It's found in relationship — with yourself, with your body, with your life as it actually is, not the version you're constantly trying to manage.

Trusting Your Response

There is a quiet shift that happens when you stop trying to control every outcome. You still care. You still act. You still grow. But you are no longer preparing for impact.

You trust yourself to respond instead of forcing a plan. You trust your body to guide you instead of not listening to it. You trust that you do not have to get everything right all at once.

That trust does not make life easy. But it makes it lighter. And when life feels lighter, you have more room to live inside it — without burning yourself out just to prove you are doing it right.

This Is What Practicing Being Alive Really Means

Practicing being alive does not mean becoming louder, busier, or more impressive. It means being more *here*. More honest. More embodied. More willing to feel what is actually happening instead of rushing past it in search of what is next.

It means choosing alignment over approval. Consistency over intensity. Truth over performance. Letting your life be something you inhabit, not something you are constantly trying to optimize or escape.

That is how a life gets lived — not perfectly, but fully.

You are Allowed to Live Now

If there is one thing I want you to take with you, it is this: you do not have to wait until everything is resolved to start living. You do not have to earn ease. You do not have to prove readiness. You do not have to become someone else first.

You are allowed to live now — inside the life you already have — with intention, presence, and care. That is not settling.

It is discernment. It is choosing to be in relationship with your life as it unfolds, instead of postponing it until you feel finished.

And that choice, practiced daily, is what changes everything.

Daily Practice: Staying With Yourself

At the end of today, pause for a moment.

Ask yourself:

Where did I stay with myself today?

Notice even one moment.

Let that count.

That is how purpose becomes livable.

That's how life stays turned up — without burning you out.

CHAPTER 13

STAY FREE

There is not a moment where this work will be finished. There is no day where you will wake up fully in control, permanently clear, and never pulled off course again.

That idea sounds comforting, but it is not real life.

Real life includes pressure. Fatigue. Old habits resurfacing when you're stretched thin. Moments where you react before you realize what is happening. Days where you move through your life without fully feeling yourself inside it.

That is not failure.

That is being human.

The practices in this book are not about never checking out. They are about not abandoning yourself when you do.

Practicing being alive doesn't mean staying perfect. It means staying present enough to return — without punishment, without stories, without turning it into a problem.

Forgetting Is Human

There will be moments when you forget what you know.

You will rush when you meant to pause. You will say yes when your body wanted to say no. You will fall back into old language, old patterns, old urgency.

Not because you didn't learn the lesson — but because stress tightens the nervous system, and tightened systems default to what feels familiar.

That does not erase your progress.

It shows you where gentleness is needed.

The difference now is subtle, but powerful. You notice sooner. You come back faster. You stop making disconnection mean something is wrong with you.

That is growth.

Nothing is finished, nothing is missing. Being alive is not something you master; it is something you practice.

Return Without Punishment

Most people turn reconnection into work. They analyze, explain, replay, and judge — and in doing so, they delay the very return they are looking for.

Returning does not require insight.

It requires contact.

When you notice you have checked out, the practice is simple:

Pause.

Name it quietly: *I left myself for a moment.*

Take one breath.

Do one regulating action.

Resume your life.

You do not need to "get back on track."

You are the track.

Containment Over Control

Power is not intensity. It is not breakthroughs. It is not transformation that looks impressive from the outside.

Power is containment.

It is the ability to stay present when things feel unfinished. To hold discomfort without turning against yourself. To move forward without performing certainty.

Each time you stay, your system learns something important: **I can be here.**

That trust compounds. It softens how you decide. It reduces the urgency to prove or protect. It builds a steadiness that does not need to announce itself.

Living the Practice

Integration is not about applying everything you learned. It is about living your life — and letting the practices show up naturally in how you pause, how you speak, how you choose, how you rest.

You do not need to remember every concept. You do not need to reference the system daily.

What matters is this:

- You notice when you leave yourself.
- You come back without punishment.
- You stay more often than you disappear.

That is enough.

That's the work.

And that's how you stay free.

Closing Practice: Stay

At the end of the day — or when you remember — pause.

Ask yourself:

Where did I stay with myself today?

It might have been:

- a boundary you did not explain.
- a breath you took instead of rushing.
- a moment of rest without guilt.
- a reaction you softened.

Notice even one moment.

Let it count.

Then say — quietly or out loud:

I'm still here.

Nothing else is required.

This is how the practice lives.

This is how trust is built.

This is how a life stays intact — without force, without burnout, without leaving.

THE END

One More Thing

You made it to the end.

Most people don't.

Most people stop at Chapter 3 because it gets uncomfortable. They go back to what they know. Back to the numbing. Back to the distractions.

You didn't.

You stayed through every chapter. Every hard truth. Every moment that probably hit a little too close to home.

That matters.

Not because this book fixed everything. Not because you have it all figured out now.

But because you showed up for yourself.

And if you can do that here, in these pages, when no one's watching and no one's grading you?

You can do it anywhere.

You can do it in that conversation you've been avoiding.

You can do it when your body says stop and your mind says push.

You can do it when old patterns try to pull you back.

You can stay.

Not perfectly. Not forever without slipping.

But more often than you disappear.

And that? **That's everything.**

That's how lives change. That's how patterns break. That's how you stop surviving and start living.

So go.

Take what you learned here and live it.

Mess it up. Forget it. Come back to it.

Just don't abandon yourself.

Stay close. Stay gentle. Stay present.

Stay free.

THE END FOR REAL THIS TIME <3

ABOUT THE AUTHOR

C.L. HURT

C.L. Hurt is an author, speaker, certified life coach, licensed massage therapist, wellness entrepreneur, and creator of **The Practice of Being Alive™** framework—a system designed to help people reconnect with themselves without burning out in the process.

She holds an Associate's Degree in Communications from Rowan University and professional certifications in life coaching and massage therapy. As the founder of **Body Needs 101**, a wellness company dedicated to helping people understand and honor what their bodies are asking for, she bridges the gap between personal development and somatic wisdom.

Her work as a humanitarian is lived, not just proclaimed—she actively serves unhoused and elderly communities through Body Needs 101, bringing therapeutic touch, presence, and dignity to those society often overlooks. She's also passionate about comprehensive sex education for young people, creating safe spaces for honest conversations about bodies, boundaries, and consent. This commitment extends beyond business—it's about creating accessible pathways to healing and knowledge, especially for communities that have been taught to override their needs or stay silent about what matters most.

Born and raised in Camden, New Jersey, C.L. knows what it means to survive. To move faster than you're ready. To carry more than you can hold. To look fine on the outside while quietly disconnecting on the inside. She's lived the patterns she writes about—the rushing, the overriding, the saying yes when the body says no.

The Power of You: Stop Surviving, Start Living is the result of years spent learning how to honor her own signals, regulate her nervous system, and build a life that doesn't require escaping. It's not a book written from the mountaintop—it's a book written from the messy middle, where most of us actually live.

C.L.'s work is grounded in **nervous system regulation, intentional living, and the practice of returning to yourself—again and again.** She doesn't teach perfection. She teaches presence. She doesn't promise overnight transformation. She offers a system that actually works when you work it.

Through her writing, speaking, and coaching, she helps people recognize the difference between effort and alignment, between forcing and flowing, between surviving and fully being alive.

Her approach is precise, systems-driven, and relentlessly honest—which makes sense when you know she's a double Virgo (Sun and Rising) with an Aries Moon. She sees patterns others miss, builds frameworks that actually work, and refuses to sugarcoat hard truths. The Virgo in her creates the structure; the Aries pushes her to say what needs to be said, even when it's uncomfortable. If you're looking for spiritual bypassing or toxic positivity, this isn't it. If you're ready for a system that meets you where you are and asks you to stay there long enough to actually integrate—this is your book.

When she's not writing or working with clients, C.L. is a mother, a student of life, and someone who still practices what she teaches—daily. Because the work of being alive isn't something you graduate from. It's something you return to, over and over, with compassion, honesty, and the courage to keep showing up.

Her belief:

You are not broken. You're not behind. You're not too much or not enough. You're human. And being human requires practice.

Her mission:

To help people stop abandoning themselves in the name of productivity, perfection, or proving their worth—and start living from the inside out.

Her hope:

That this book becomes the permission slip you didn't know you needed. That it meets you exactly where you are. And that it reminds you of something you already know but maybe forgot:

You're allowed to be here. You're allowed to rest. You're allowed to receive. You're allowed to live—not just survive.

This is the practice.

This is the life.

This is the power of you.

www.ingramcontent.com/pod-product-compliance
Ingram Content Group UK Ltd.
Pitfield, Milton Keynes, MK11 3LW, UK
UKHW012249290726
14090UKWH00013B/544

9 798994 701300